ISBN 978-1-105-24362-2

EXORCISING MY DAEMONS

A JOURNEY INTO ONE MAN'S SOUL

MICHAEL S. SLOCUM

ISBN 978-1-105-24362-2

ACKNOWLEDGEMENTS

I would like to dedicate this book to my wife, Leora. Without her I would not have love. Without her I would not have a partner. Without her I would not have my son, Micaiah, or my daughter, Hosannah. Without the three of them, I would have nothing.

Without her I would not have daemons- but the daemons make the man. And exorcising those daemons make a song. As you read this collection of poems- you will hear my song.

My experiences and passions intersect in a space of despair and hope. Mixed together and distorted with wonder and dread. Sorrow and hope crash together like waves from two different storms. There is no winner. But there is insight. There is insight into one man's soul.

FORWARD

Out of the quarrels of our life we make rhetoric; out of the quarrels with ourselves we make poetry."

--W.B. Yeats

Anyone who has ever been compelled to capture an idea and imprison it on paper has some grasp of what it means to exorcise a daemon. Whether the compulsion is deemed positive or negative, it is somehow a catharsis to put pen to paper (or fingers to keys) and pour out a thought, a desire or an imagining to the priest that is Poetry. By sharing his resolve, the poet allows his reader to experience a type of release as well. In *Exorcising My Daemons*, Michael Slocum's first poetry collection, we are invited in as he wrestles his spirits of loss and love, futility and hope.

Michael, whose previous works include books, articles and seminars on problem solving and innovation, has built a livelihood and reputation on identifying answers where others find none. With his poetry he continues his endeavor of answer seeking, but with an approach more soulful than practical. Rather than presenting solutions, Michael provides his reader the stimulus and opportunity for pondering life's beautifully complicated questions.

Michael has numerous passions, both personally and professionally; with fascinating work experiences, travels and studies too numerous to mention. With laser-like focus and the ability to devour information unlike anyone else I have known, he has developed a vast knowledge base on a myriad of topics. As is so often the case, art imitates life. Michael's wide array of interests provides poetic influences ranging from The Pixies to Poe, and subject matter from artificial intelligence to sweaters. From the light-hearted "Missy Aggravation", to the Latin-based "Vox Demonic" series, to the Greek-influenced "Persephone and the Dragon" Michael embraces the full spectrum of human emotion and substance. While never losing sight of his convictions, he blends history, science and mythology to subtly illuminate our human complexities. His themes are universal – good vs. evil; honesty vs. deceit; hope vs. doubt – but never simplistic. Poetry speaks to the heart; Michael's speaks equally to the mind.

When my dear friend invited me to pen the foreword of this book, I briefly questioned his judgment. Typically, introducing a poet's first published collection is a task reserved for a critic, a professor of literature, or perhaps a world-renowned author. I am none of these. I am, however, someone who delights in getting lost in elegant words on a page; who marvels at the poet's ability to delicately string hard science around a broken heart; who loves stumbling across a well-worded phrase that perfectly captures a moment. If you possess these same qualifications, then I'll detain you no longer. It's time to indulge yourself in the quest for truth, or dragons, or absolution -- whatever your daemons may be.

Melissa Thacker

Here There Be Dragons

Melissa Thacker

When you've arrived at the end of all that you know

And find yourself still seeking;

Press on if you must,

But know in your lust

The dragons will be creeping.

When in your freedom you seek to forge a new path,

The way is always winding.

Promising doors there

Untrodden ground where

With care you loose your binding.

Unguarded and free now to seek hidden treasure

The dragon will search your face.

Gaze into your eyes,

See through all your lies

Plotting while you test the grace.

Opened minds are dragons' prey; a double-edged sword

Required to be enlightened.

Yet they set the snare

And they lead you where

Your path be dark'd or brightened.

You pray your reward fully merits the danger –

The thrill will equal the price.

You'll return unscarred

Or broken and marred

Freedom alone will suffice.

And what will become of the new love you find?

Is charity best hidden?

Love conquers the rules

Destroys all the tools

Questions all that's forbidden.

When you've come to the end of all that you know

And continue on still seeking –

A cleft in the road,

New truths to be told

And the dragons will be creeping.

Persephone and the Dragon

Her hair was ebonne darkness but it dazzled like Arcturus. Her eyes were wells of soulfull longing and were too much for man to gaze. Her countenance shown like one thousand suns and she smelled of roses and lavender. When she passed your mind was swept away. A simple thought of her would visit joy on gloomy sorrow. And when she came your way—you'd pray she'd stay until the morrow.

Although simple to see the reasons why-it is difficult to explain the hold she had on me. And the poetry that is Persephone weaves in and out of the dragon's main as the tale is told. And as it reaches culmination—her hold on me enfolds. She means the world and everything in it—but that doesn't seem enough. So if we add the universe that almost sums it up. Her voice is like the waves that crash softly on the sand. And her silver lips draw you close like the moon pulling on the water's surface. The wind touches her body and gently caresses each curve before it continues on its course. Can you imagine her glory and her becoming?

The serpent of yesteryear scratches the onyx stone and sends sparks to and fro in time with the swishing of its tail. Its tongue flicks quickly between its teeth as it tastes the air. Puffs of noxious gas escape its nostrils with each heavy breath. And all the while the stirred aroma has the taste of death. Each step draws a shudder from the heavy earth and if you watch the trembling flowers you can foretell the beast's great and mighty girth. And it causes you to tremble. Tremble with a freight so primordial you cannot yield a scream, but only hope with clench-ed jaw this somehow is a dream.

The beast seems forlorn if you match its' gaze and you can tell from scar and wound the number, of its' days. The mighty dragon is adored—but not by man or beast or any creature of the realm. But by the Gods who share with it the origin of the land. The foul beast seeks to and fro whom it may devour and if you tempt to try the beast, you will see your final hour. Can you imagine her glory and her becoming?

Her walk reminded many of the sway of grain, as in the amber fields we played upon when we were young in the land. Her laugh played out across the scape with the timbre of the flute, and mesmerized we all became as she sung us summer tunes. My Persephone was magnificent and majestic to behold- she was the source of joy and hope and reason for story told. Her hair moved like a dandelion given by the wind a start- never quite together and never quite apart. Watching her is like watching children playing in a stream, where the brook is bubbling over rock and mists their faces to keep them cool.

She listens like you are the only sound ever to be heard and her face makes you feel she wants to understand all your words. One against the world it seems but infinite by her side. I long to be with Persephone, does she long to be with me? She knows the time is coming soon where our fates intertwine—where the glory of the maiden fair becomes a child of mine. And when we speak of these lofty concepts, in earnest be they true-there is no purer love to be had-then the love from me to her. Can you imagine her glory and her becoming?

A mighty roar drives the raven from the tree, the beast is on the prowl and other creatures flee. The power from the broken solitude is like a gaping wound cut new. The beast thrashes through brush and thicket, driving closer and closer to you. You can feel death standing the hairs on your neck. As your pace quickens you know you cannot escape. The beast has come for you and you will succumb to your final fate. Crash! The stony ground crumbles beneath each mighty gait of the beast. The dragon senses victory and acceptance of your fate. Determination flees your limbs and you feel the cracking of your bones as the teeth of trepidation meet, ending the flicker of your soul. Can you feel the glory of her becoming?

I meet her gaze and I know it is a dream. My corporal self is ever sundered and this cannot be what it seems. She holds me gently as only Persephone can and as she whispers in my ear, I sense a wholeness once again. I feel my fate flee the bedside of my doom- and ever softly I hear my maiden sing the loveliest of tunes,

"Can you see the glory of my becoming? Can you feel the whisper of my love? Can you sense the magic of our fondness? Can you feel the magic in my touch? My love for you will reproach the dragon and draw your spirit free. So as you hear my whispered song—return my love, and be with me."

The dragon let me fall from her mouth, broken and my body torn. What was once a living being crumpled to the cold ground and my hope bled into puddles at the feet of the beast. Somehow I didn't feel cold or pain. Only the soft hum of Persephone's voice coursed through my mind. She was gorgeous to behold and I was enthralled by her as I could not be by death. From near or far she held the gaze of all and defeated the dark lord's hold on me. Her beauty shimmered as if her countenance were wind-swept. And she had me completely in death as she had in life. Can you imagine her glory and her becoming?

As I passed from gruesome death into glorious life, I sensed a truth that had escaped me time and time again. The tail of the beast had that ebonne sheen that shimmered down the back of my Perspehone. Her eyes could glow like embers as the eyes of the mighty beast. And all nature bowed to her wonder as it did in fear of the dragon once unleashed. Intertwined as one from beginning and for eternity, Persephone is the Dragon after all. Can you imagine her glory and her becoming?

Braids of Aphrodite

To twist the hair of Aphrodite
On the shores of lovely Cyprus
When the moon is full and waves crash softly near
Is a dream of mine

Love, desire, and beauty in each strand
Smooth to touch and look upon
Like the sands of Egypt before Octavianus
Strands of silken sympathy

It isn't just to touch but to feel
Each weave makes us closer to the other
A gentle touch with powerful movements
Venus in a tapestry of love and lust

Each pass weaves another wave in the ocean of passion
A crescendo of feeling poised on romance and lust
A golden arrow waiting to pierce his mind and body
Loving her in Demeter like Eros did Aphrodite

Each motion releases the scent of her beauty
Braids of affection pour down her back
By his hands were they made
And his desire makes them perfectly wound

Adonis and Myrrha together at night
Their Son cared for by Persephone
Whose hair is a braid of golden luster
Made from mornings of togetherness

Accompanied by Charites in love and war
Braiding her hair to knot his desire there
His fingers feeling her softly and at once
Leaving her mesmerized as he pulls and weaves

Aphrodite rides the Swan as he touches her hair
Each quick motion bringing to an end
The interlacing hold he has on her
Only to begin again when the knots are loosed

Winds and tides shake the foundation
But the knots are safe until his hands loose them
Only to smooth her hair
And knot it again-every day the same way

Galatea caught his gaze with a braid of ivory wonder
A gift from Aphrodite- of words and imaginations
Spurring his love to lofty heights
And gentle mornings of a lover's consecration

The Judgment of Paris seen in the tapestry of her woven
hair
An apple for the fairest one from Eris to the Goddesses
Paris of Troy to make the choice, appointed by Zeus
He won Helen from Aphrodite's promise

Helen's hair is braided daily and her lover's touch is sure
He finds her in a waking dream, and she finds him, as it
were
Time touches all it seems- a kiss of eternal enmity
Braids of love bind them fast it seems- in exact proximity

Simultaneous

In the reign of Mithridates Magus
O feared enemy of Rome
Two souls where as one so as not to be alone
Under watch of Mother Laodice
He shared with her his home

Under sword of Pompey fell Mithridates
Though poison passed his lips
Rome was safe again
His hands never parted from her hips
Lucilia held his desires at bay with the same strength

The words of Tacitus record their love
In annals time has kept
Preserved each look and longing touch
For others to regret
The Germania tells the tale

Flames unyielding from a lover's look
A touch lingers beyond propriety
Strawberries stain the stomach
And Plutarch has many lives
He would live each one with you

Blood on her lips from a lover's bite
Or maybe Nyx, Goddess of the Night
Weaving in and out of a lover's embrace
Her primordial aura sates his taste
Like a story from Hesiod's Theogony

Love's phylactery weighs me down
Ardent mantle and lofty crown
Warming my body by day
At night crumpled on the ground
In a heap of realization

Night is borne of Chaos
And the tempest holds her soul
He holds her arms apart and there her heart
Bared and in his hold
His desire raises the phoenix from the ashes
As she watches him from half-closed lashes

Aristophanes' Birds inspire Orphic perambulation
As he moves on a path of satisfaction
Her hands in his as he placates without distraction
Loving her above his nation's safety
Like Paris did Helen, so long ago

Son of Ares and Aphrodite at their side
Urging culmination in the heavens
Love before lusty abomination
And pageantry in the shadows and whispers
In the room and on the floor

Together as one- Apollo and Daphne
The arrow of lusty fate pierced them both
Killing them as one- a death that was at most
Sanctimonious
A death that was at least
Simultaneous

Fourteen Minutes

Fourteen minutes was not enough
To touch the sky they needed time
Seconds passed quickly while they danced
As they moved to Orphic chant and rhyme

Zeus and Persephone- intertwined
In Hellenistic romance under Sun and Moon
On the table of Olympus dined
He feeds her grapes and dandelions

From Hades he rescues her each day
Soft hands pull her free from death
He kisses away webs of Alexander
And dresses her in robes of alabaster

The seconds pass quickly while they danced
The tune changes as does the wind itself
Passing from sorrow to sinful and back again
Seconds passing as the wind through leaves

Their pace quickens noticeably
Hounds approach from East and West
He holds her tight as she does he
The pressure mounts and leads to stress

Chariots pass drawn by horses of fire
He mourns the loss of time so dire
Draws her kisses to replace his ire
Kindled passion moving higher

The seconds pass quickly while they danced
Moved together in heliocentric romance
Eurydice passes and leaves another
Youthful lover in her place

Heavens shatter in a cascade of fierce emanations
He moves under her declarations
Cause and effort mightily won
The time has passed and they have none

He is Paris and she is Helen
Taken from Menelaus by fate
And passion and love unconquered
The time slips by vanquished from their side

The seconds pass quickly while they danced
1000 ships hold afloat their romance
Fleeting, Fleeting, Fleeting
Their hearts are beating

The lovers yield- time has left them alone with their heat
In the tempest of unfinished promises
Swirling in a sea of honest turmoil
Fourteen minutes was not enough

Verisimilitude

I've never met her but I don't need to
She reaches out to me with word and deed
And thoughts of verisimilitude
A touch like that is as real as any other
And I know she speaks to me
I hear her voice when I need to
Our bond is laced with everlasting
And knotted with infinite understanding
We are together though we are apart
We share a waking dream
The two of us

I've never kissed her but I don't need to
The wave of emotion from that touch
Comes to me anyway
And I am washed in peace and comfort when it does
She has that hold on my soul
But it is a gentle touch
We know each other
And our bond is implacable
We are together though we are apart

We share a waking dream
The two of us

I've never held her but I don't need to
I hold her time and her attention
With interactions sublime
In a place-I am hers and she is mine
She occupies my thoughts in many certain ways
She has a place in my composition
And her beauty lights my days
She fixes my gaze like the dominant star
On our life's horizon
And only her
Shall I forever keep my eyes on

I'll never love another the way that I love her
And that's the way it should be
We share a waking dream
The two of us

Heather

Heather in the field and on the screen
Watch her lips- see what she means
Passing fancy in my dreams
But Heather isn't what she seems

Vampire girl living in the city
Black hair like death but very pretty
Passing memory and terrible screams
But Heather isn't what she seems

Red eyes and lies and hidden pride
Fears and sleeping by your side
Love letters flow in feverish reams
But Heather isn't what she seems

Love and trepidation
A mortal man in an immortal nation
Blood boils and sweat steams
But Heather isn't what she seems

Anthracite

Your heart and soul glisten in the moonlight
Bared and cleaved as disgorged anthracite
Alone and scared at midnight
You hope and pray it's all right
And then you lose your site

You can sense the breath as the beast approaches
But you are unable to react
On your back for the last attack
It comes in waves of anguish

It all passes as does the fright
Liquid red and cold anthracite
Dropped love fractures scattering the light
Of the life leaving your eyes
No one dies and then cries

You can sense the breath as the beast approaches
But you are unable to react
On your back for the last attack
It comes in waves of anguish

You have been found guilty of covenants with the devil

Your ministry reeks of death and rancor
You taste guile and blood with wicked canker
Rancid rambling as you murmur
Fate will leave your fetid feelings
At the door of tomorrow's disenchantment

Feeling like you've done this before
On another planet behind a different door
Acid rain waters anthracnose
There is your hope and there it goes

You have been found guilty of covenants with the devil

Phoebe, Our Springer Spaniel

Hey- she looked so small next to her brothers and sisters
And the box she slept in was much too big for her
But her heart was larger than any other
And she loved us with it every day
For fourteen years she was by our side
Chasing birds and squirrels and rabbits
Springing off our wall, a proud example of her breed
We will always recall her smile and her playful ways
Her restlessness and stubborn loyalty
Her sisters will miss her as we will
But we know she is in a flowered field
Under the sun
At a full sprint- ears flying behind her
A squirrel just out of reach
And she couldn't be happier
Hey- we will never forget our beloved dog

Chelsea

Fanciful and presently tense
In a world replete with love and good intentions
She should have lived forever

Angelic manifestation
Of what should be and where hope perseveres
She should have survived his temptation

Light dancing on the water's surface
Where the wind kisses the waves before they crash
She should have loved and that love lasted

The sun refracts love into a myriad of actions
When passion and patience reside without distraction
She should have worn a white dress in satisfaction

Music comforting those who feel the vibrations
As joy and warmth pass over us in oscillations
She should have smiled away her mother's consternation

Arcing wayward in darkest sorrow
Passing the place where hope lay barren
She should have woken sleepy eyed tomorrow

Pitching foreword into the twisting nether
Catching hearts as she clutched the air
She could have lived forever

Her eyelids flutter when she dreams and weeps
The breeze sends ripples through her hair
She should be peaceful as she sleeps

SELFISH

You sit and stare directly ahead
Alive outside and inwardly dead
Pretending truth from the things you've read
Branded "selfish" across your forehead

The rain drops drown it out
Pitter patter unending shout
Liquid torrent and then it ends
Blown away by westward winds

Cast aside- tempest subsiding
In the open and no longer hiding
Clawed marks from the past
Open wounds that eternally last

Unable to pass it by
You stare mistake dead in the eye
White to white and black to black
Deep in despair- no turning back

You did it for yourself with anger and malice
Directed inward and so intense
The past snapped around your waist
And tore into your breast

The blood pours out with your future
Cold- you look into the sky
And the same blank reflection you've seen before
Mirrors sadness in your eyes

And the Wings Glow Brightly Red

And the Wings Glow Brightly Red

Fear hovers near with wisps of worry

The flutter of the demon bird can be heard

And the wings glow brightly red

As it hovers overhead

Afraid to look and see the hoary cry of abandon

Waiting to be screamed in my face

My eyes stay tight and I murmur prayers

To one who cares and hope he deigns to act

Red glow playing on my face

Ancient messenger patient for my attention

Unholy end or holy intervention

If only I were brave enough to look

Temper and Dispassion

The best you can do is stare at the place where he stood

Imagine you see his smile directed your way

Imagine you can hear his laugh roll quite easily

The future is a hard and cold master

And it has found you alone and lost

A victim of your temper and dispassion

As you host selfishness and sickness to a seat

At the table of your heart

There to keep and sleep in each other's arms

Tears recall how you used to be

When soft and caring meant something

And cold and staring was locked deep in the winter of your despair

But you don't feel the burn of concern

If love can't make a home – hate will do just fine

The Flight of the Honeybee

The flight of the honeybee looks erratic

At first glance and consideration

Knowing the intent to spread beauty and grace

Underlies wisdom in this vision

So not the pace or route she takes

But more closely the beauty she recuperates

The honeybee flies for you

The flight of the honeybee is not her own

Like the mother she has other goals

Service to others before self

As the wind blows for the rain and not for gain

A gentle touch and a kiss and she is gone

The flowers bend towards her in anticipation

Others like them will be grown

The flight of the honeybee duplicates

That erstwhile curve of a sky full of light

By day or night she plays her part

In God's effervescent plan of color and aromatic wonder

Guiding victory to sight and smell

Her senses serve so well

As does the sting she guards with life

Only without understanding

Does she seem without plan

Those that look and know

See the beauty and understand

She flies for you and she flies for me

She changes the world with a touch

The honeybee blesses and gives so much

Binary Enemies

In rotation about a common center of mass

The future leads the past

In a curved transgression inside our mind

Friend and enemy intertwined

An x-ray eclipse brings calm before the storm

As magnificent radiation is the norm

Passing in periodicity you and I

Enemy or friend we are in the same horizon

Poison temptation draws you in

And escape is not possible

The event horizon leaves no way out

So together we spin

Rotating enemies and friends

Cacophony

The way the world moves with a background noise

Tells you we are a people of anger

Crash and clang above the din

Hearing repressed fear as we spin into sin

Doppler shifting to and from the center of a friendly
world

Equal mass unequal trepidation

We rise in waves as a liquid nation

Our burdens clank together like dishes in a sink

We listen for breaking china

While we dream of fears and think

We find an inner Lagrangian point and idle at peace

Waiting for war to shatter the balance

The cacophony tears down my face

Converted to liquid loss and traces my future on my skin

And as I taste the salt I fade away

I am gone as the waves of sound die down

A Bird Trapped in a Cage

The world will kill you
The world terrorizes you
The world will crush you
Danger all around you
Mayhem and it comes for you
Manson and his family too
The world kills its young
Communism killing Christ
Religions abound in sight
The apocalypse will come one night
Jihad near and coming soon
Fire and flame burns around you
The world measures you
Immolation for a godless desire
Death silently calls
A red dawn comes for us all
Evil evil everywhere
Death comes from above
There is no room for hope or love
Satan on unholy cross
Zodiacal perversion of the Mazzeroth

Atheism fills the air
Hypocrite zombies everywhere
Detonations fill the air
Hate, fear, and then despair
The bomb that ends it all
Selfish desires come first
Murder comes for those who wake
Holocaust the others take
Perversion of the senses
Abuse of the soul
Extreme hatred for the living
Communism taking hold
The shelved lives of young and old
Destruction when you least expect
Fear never dormant in this place
Crying eyes and anguished tears
The guns, the guns, the guns and fears
Do you feel like a bird trapped in a cage?
Dictatorial hatred and rage
Tormented souls at every age
Despise! Despise! Despise!
Nuclear death and so many lies
War against peace and humanity

Drugs to cause persistent insanity
Worlds collide and shake
Famine and sorrow for all to take
Divorce and matrimonial suffering
Even good deeds end in agony
Burning complete destruction
Four horsemen kill with abandon
Anguish and absolution
Humanism and corruption
The world lies to you
The enemy despises you
Gambling taxes you
Grief breaks you in two
The sun can crush and devastate
Hatred is so commonplace
She cries with evil in her place
Selfish desires her soul to take
Satan in his habitat
And the enemy is fine with that
gods and gods and gods abound
Death above and on the ground
Do nothing and die
Alone not alive

Rubble covers all the lies
The world curses you
Burns your heart in two
Do you feel like a bird trapped in a cage?
Nuclear rage
Deceit is lord of this age
No food to eat
Soulless fears to keep
Islam gives the world no sleep
And the world comes to an end
Takes away your friends
Frozen pain again, again
The truth is always far from us
Mixing lies and lust with lack of trust
Vilest bird waiting for us
The world cries "disobedience"
The waters spin and spin for us
We scream but who cares to hear?
Pain and suffering always near
The ground would swallow us
Depraved men want to eat at us
Pain is the name of the game
Conflict from sin again and again

This devil boy is no one's friend
Maniacal men from end-to-end
Take your life you have no friends
Baby killers at every door
Marching madmen- Satan's whore
At any age they kill for sport
Liars white and black
They'll eat your flesh- unholy attack
Millions dead and dying
For lies and those who are lying
Bound and held
Left for dead
Split in two—your heart, your head
Your ship is sinking
Your head is spinning
You're selfish and you aren't winning
Broken Siva still grinning
Evil leading
Uncivil bleeding
Hope receding
Your void is reeling
Crime has meaning
Brutally demeaning

And Satan feeding
Your work enslaves you more
The lies are even worse than before
The sun hates us all
Red dawn and then the fall
War machines ground bone to dust
Love is captured- replaced with lust
Death surrounds you
Those that would will kill you
You cannot trust a godless world
The fire and flames they come for you
Who will stand when the others are gone?
Crosses burn and white is wrong
Immorality in every place
Demonic grin on every face
Food no longer commonplace
Lies by the Father of Lies
This baby's doom is stainless
And pagan death is painless
A plague of immorality
Radiation and contemplation
Do you feel like a bird trapped in a cage?
Are you lost- as in a maze?

On the tracks train spotting for days
Dead end and dead life
Filled with booze, drugs, and strife
A slippery slope and then the knife
Bleeding heart with walls and broken dolls
A gun to your head
But you're not dead
Apathy and abandon
Satan devours at will and random
Guilt—the great equalizer
You need another tranquilizer
The flood comes for you
In blood and stone
They'll take your hope and burn your home
She has a light but is so alone
Heresy and heretic
So much sin to make you sick
You are damaged and without value
Armageddon comes for you
He screams and she dies slow
Hitler was not that long ago
Rape and control
Narcissism and your soul

Godless life and eternal strife
Sin and sinned against for life
Deluge comes but leaves the dirt
Neglect and wrecked and hurt
The lake of fire is what you'll get
Fake is even better yet
Pressure and force
Do for yourself of course
Cynicism the way of life
Promiscuity and discontinuity
Common man uncommon evil
Torture and immoral brutality
Greed and all the other sins
You hate yourself and have no friends
Despair but you don't care
The baby she wishes wasn't there
Fate comes and you have no control
The mask hides your smile and soul
The world's god is not in control
You all even look the same
Share the same defective brain
You want it now or not at all
Yes- that's your blood on the wall

Coexist and surrender

The world is your cage, it has nothing for you

Obsidian Baphomet

~~Inspired by a dream told to me by Melissa Young Cline~~

Dagon laps the waters and the waves
Blood and fury in the froth
Underwater pantheon
Waits obsidian megaloth

She feels the weight of the water on her chest
And in this dream she finds no rest

Messianic undercurrent
Legs of iron and feet of stone
She waits upon a maiden sacrifice
Nearer coming to the throne

She tastes the blood mixed with the water
Hearing the gloom in Satan's laughter

Crashing tempest unholy shout
Ships and wreckage all about
Broken bodies are afloat
Underneath the iron a leg of goat

Her lips turn up in frightful glimmer
All around the basest sinners

Truth and beauty flee to peace
Panic widens awakes the beast
Obsidian pantheon ever dancing
Blackest hate and necromancy

Blue is her face as she tastes tightening fear
She tries to scream but none can hear

She fears in tears for quickest succor
There is none to hear and it is not met
Cept by the baleful hateful gaze
Of dreaded Obsidian Baphomet

Cords of corruption hold her fast
This weakened breath will be her last

Cloven hoof of ebon splendor
Sharpest dagger long and slendor
Quickest entry not to error
The blood it flows unleashing terror

She feels the pain of death inside
Tenses white as her eyes go wide

Abomination and desecration
Red and thick is the blood moon water
Destroyed avenged and left for dead
Lies loveliest of Freedom's daughters

My Favorite Mistake

Time stands still and watches me weep
Passing by with earnest sympathy
Watching all my err and weakness
Surrounded by a weak frivolity

Chortle whence my anger came
It wasn't me despite the blame
She wasn't mine to try to take
Her heart aligned for me to break

Deepest ponder in submission
As I wonder at my folly
Loving her was just a mission
Sending in another volley

Splashing wonder all I wanted
To attack and draw asunder
Wider still we passed affronted
There it was- magnificent blunder

A spray of remorse and coldest sorrow
You cannot keep and you cannot borrow
Set her free for her return
Cry all night and try to learn

Life is full of give and take
You rise and fall and fix and break
And in your failure reflecting fondly
Oft recall precious mistake

O to be Poseidon

Aphrodite sitting on the stone
Sprayed by water but not alone
Sun kissed maiden o so fair
Rays of light in her golden hair
O to be Poseidon when she bathes

Energetic pulse and warmth
Her smile heats ocean waves
Her words make peace in the universe
Minutes by her side like longest days
O to be Poseidon when she bathes

Truth and beauty call her name
Apollyon flees at sight
Mornings in her loving embrace
Call forth for gentle night
O to be Poseidon when she bathes

Outside an angel descends to earth
Draped in whispers and a fog
Look upon her while you can

She has no other analogue
O to be Poseidon when she bathes

all you are

quantify your horror
maximize your loss
distribute your sorrow
turn the tv off

spell the name of satan
mouth the fear you feel
drive away from family
drink behind the wheel

skip the time together
pretend you do not know
look the other way
focus on the picture show

bleat when asked a question
lie when you don't know
follow any leader
just a tax don't you know?

And the Waves All Look the Same

It is so very dark outside
The sun has fled and tried to hide
The scape seems so very strange
Our opened eyes find the world deranged

The night comes stretched and pale
Stars constant when they shine
While Luna waits inside her vale
And bides her time to speak her mind

Listen quietly to the whisper and hear
From her lips and through the trees
Her dying breath is very near
Dancing with hope and dying leaves

The snow came and covered the tale
Luna wept into the earth that day
The tracks are gone with all detail
We had much hope but couldn't stay

Stellar bound singing wonderful
Cosmic echo of hope and fear
Red planet lies behind it all
Another chance we hold so dear

When it is fall we fall
When it is dead we die
When we grope for Luna
We make her cry

Red tears to track our fate
Imprinted and traced from now until yesterday
We walk each time during the day
And it ends again in the same way

Santayana fell and traveled well
First astronaut from Egyptian lore
He's seen it all as he has before
He fled the future and came ashore

And the waves all look the same
And the waves all look the same

Hallelujah

Worlds collide and so will ours
With a future state that we create
Parallel lost and can't be found
It spins and spins
And we go 'round

Maybe there is a God above
As stars fall from his hand
Does he watch them in lost love?
Does he see just where they land?
Hallelujah

The night comes and the storm is close
The rope is cut and so is hope
Pitch and yaw we fret and claw
We slide and cry the jagged slope
Hallelujah

The icy rancor weakens spirit
Made the only world our whore
Love and lust and loss and fear
Cannot save us anymore
Hallelujah

Coiling hope at destiny's door
Like a bridge to a better tomorrow
But when we descend the depths of will
All we find is coldest sorrow
Hallelujah

All those feelings merely mortal
Heaven help us if she can
When we sleep in tempest mourning
Save us and then save our land
Hallelujah

Dark Sky and Eyes of Blue

There you are standing in the wind
Gleaming eyes taking in my sin
Rose lips bitten blood is flowing
Warmth engulfing as the fire is growing

Venus low in the sky and moving fast
Curving the present to the past
We hold our hands- watch the slowest ark
Kiss upon kiss in the growing dark

Juxtaposition and collide
Volcanic eruption but I'm by your side
Spinning in eternal orbit true
The sky is dark but your eyes are blue

The sun will come in the morning brightly
Exposing blushing lovers rightly
Pausing perfect in the balance
Plain as day are all your talents

Transmission

I've lost control of this transmission
Through rampant terror and indecision
I tried to find another mission
But it just wasn't there for me

Stellar cold capitulation
Aeons pass in indignation
Hesiod's eternity in blue
That's the color best for you

Blood red the moon
Stars blink silent agreement
Leave the ledge at once
Start your descent into the twilight

Sublime all the time
She floats in the Milky Way
Billowing in vacuum
Silent and beautiful

I've lost control of this transmission
Plato's ideological indecision
Sacramental is the mission
But it just wasn't there for me

Bloody moon and a blue dress
Twilight as you undress
Leave the edge at once
Descend into darkness with a warm heart

Cooling Quickly and Aloof

Sunlight glimmers on the petals
Of the flower as the wind gently
Touches it and then moves on
Playing across another flower
Nearby but far away
If you consider the journey it has taken
To live and grow where it does
Under the same sunlight
And in the same wind
But different as day from night

Moonlight dances across the water
Waves are pulled up by the touch
Of its ardent lunar lover
White are the caps as if smiling in response
To the gentle kiss and caress
Of so lonely a lady
Waltzing heavenly and nodding in our direction
Glowing at night perpetually
In constant affection
Following the sun each day as if connected

Different but connected

Day and Night

Dark and Light

Playing and dancing

Over water and on the petals of a flower

Day by day and hour by hour

Night follows quickly and the seconds pass

It is all dust and embers

Crushed but red from passion

Cooling quickly and aloof

Scent in the Air was Rare

She approached from behind
He was rocking slowly and mumbling to himself
He seemed unaware of her presence
But his rocking slowed imperceptibly
Whatever kept him company knew she was near
And she stepped back in fear
She began to speak but paused to search her words
His head tilted slightly as if he knew
She would speak to them soon
His rocking increased and she saw drops of blood on the
wood
Dripping from his wrists onto the floor
She stepped back again- closer to the door
The scent in the air was rare
Fear boiled down to what would be left
And then burned and burned
Black as hatred and filling the air
It filled the room although still very rare
She asked about the blood
She asked about the aroma of fear and death
His rocking never paused

And his words mixed with his breath
She moved closer to hear his response
And never saw the dagger in his fist
He was smiling and showing all his teeth

Our Last Station

The world spins and life goes on
We see people we know or knew
And we say words we have said before
All the while we wonder if this is really all there is
Terse love and emancipation
Is the grave our last station?

Stigmata

We wear the scars of life
On our face and in our heart
We bleed the tears
Pierced and dragged
Through Life and Death

Pater noster, qui es in caelis,
Protect us from those who'd destroy us
sanctificetur nomen tuum.
Stay with me at night and in my room
Adveniat regnum tuum.
The bell tolls but for whom?
Fiat voluntas tua, sicut in caelo et in terra.
Come for me and those I love
Panem nostrum quotidianum da nobis hodie,
Pull us from hell and help us rise above
et dimitte nobis debita nostra
One- take control of me
sicut et nos dimittimus debitoribus nostris.
Two- it's the enemy
Et ne nos inducas in tentationem,
Let me take a ride by myself

sed libera nos a malo.

Crash into a private hell

Quia tuum est regnum, et potentia, et Gloria,

in secula.

Rescued by another life

Amen.

The world spins and life goes on

We hear sounds we used to hear

And we remember all those things that came before

We hear the creak and the slam of the door

The room is cold and I'm alone

Left to feel dark rumination

Is the grave our last station?

Stigmata

We wear the scars of life

On our face and in our heart

We bleed the tears

Pierced and dragged

Through Life and Death

Keep the Door Open

Melancholy dreams leave the door open
A light shines the way to the corner
I don't go there for fear it lurks
As it did long ago and once before
When it growled and slammed the door
The marks from claws and teeth
Hurt me deep when the lightning strikes
Driving the quake into my room
And my bed levitates with each crack
I feel the claws rake my bloody back
The sheet sticks and dries to my skin
Has it come in? Has it come in?
I can sense its eyes burning into me
But it cannot see – it cannot see
Torment has blinded the beholder
Something must have come for it
When it was a little boy
And the dark corner held its secret
Pain and death, there is no joy
Anguish has ripped compassion from its very soul

It comes for me – It comes for me
The door is shut for good this time

Saints and Sinners

Saints and sinners eating the flesh
Of the beast known as remorse
Tasting rancor and divorce in equal measures
Separating what was from what could have been
And the enemies from the friends
The table is full as are the bellies
Of the constrained angel and beast
No bones left untouched
When the wicked come to feast
The cloth is stained with pain
And anger drawn as the skin across a drum
Taught and fraught with the fear
Remembrance brings to all or none
Saints and sinners – hand in hand
One will sit while the other stands

Bellem Letale

Aggression runs under the skin
Like a subsurface wave
Always there but mostly silent
The tide comes and awakens
White froth and emanations
Pulling humanity down to the core
Hot and fluid the lava roars
Can you see the tyranny in man?
The ruin scratched into the land
Aggression runs under the skin
Where to begin – where to begin
When it starts it doesn't end
Bellum letale – we know so well
The blast it lasts forever more
We all suffer loss and destruction
When aggression manifests itself as war

Blood and Snow

Snow melts when it touches sorrow
Runs as tears down your cheek
When you think about tomorrow
Cherry blossom bleeding hollow
Screams unheard in the night
Sensing fevered pain and anguish
All things are not good or right
Blood and snow mixing at my feet
A shadow mutes the beauty
The sun crossing overhead
Slow but certain about its duty
Sadness blossoms at night
Red petals covered with midnight snow
The moon dances twinkling her light across the white
Revealing my footprints as I go
The path is long and she won't wait for long
But I must go to her while the pain is young
The wind howls against his progress
With each step forcing rest
Screaming "red planet" he remembers the time
The tears dried blood red on his face

There was no wind then- to hold him up

He moved in rhythm with wanderlust

Ancient emanations pulsed in time

In vacuum the echoes filled his mind

And still he is no closer to her

She passed by him with her own frozen sorrow

Driven by the cold and bloody rain

Covered in her deepest pain

She looked warm and afraid if he but saw

His tears would renew their flow

Maybe if he survives

He can try again tomorrow

The blood and snow comes every day

In this world not so far away

Marsquake

Screaming "red planet"
The tears dry blood red on his face
There is no wind to hold him up
He moves in rhythm with wanderlust
Ancient emanations pulse in time
In vacuum the echoes fill his mind

Molten iron ejects erratic
As the planet vibrates and hums in static
Swelling terror causes panic
Leaving hope confused and abandoned
Gamma rays impacting random
As hope fades it leaves him stranded

Galactic loss and forlorn tremors
Telling all that it remembers
Broken past and shattered present
Olympus Mons is taking credit
Shielding me from her brazen stare
Melting in the lava's glare

Tharsis holds him ever fast
Reddest doom and neverlast

Creeping lanquid indecision
Magma forms his Martian prison
Screaming "red planet" once again
He sees Earth set before the end

Vox Demonic: The Pretense

Translation for the Latin in this poem:

Vade, Satana, inventor et magister
(Go away, Satan, the inventer and master)
Omnis fallaciae, hostis humanae salutis
(Of all deceit, the enemy of humanity's salvation)
Humiliare sub potenti manu dei,
(Be humble under the powerful hand of God)
Contremisce et effuge, invocato a
(Tremble and flee — I envoke by)
Nobis sancto et terribili nomine,
(Us the sacred and terrible name)
Quem inferi tremunt
(At which those down below tremble)
Ab insidiis diaboli, libera nos, Domine
(From the snares of the devil, free us, Lord)
Ut Ecclesiam tuam secura tibi facias libertate servire
(So that you may make your Church safe to serve you freely)
Te rogamus, audi nos
(We ask you, hear us)
Ut inimicos sanctae Ecclesiae humiliare digneris

(So that you may destroy the enemies of your sacred Church)

Vade, Satana, inventor et magister
Shackle me in Hell and keep me there
Omnis fallaciae, hostis humanae salutis
The Prince of Darkness torments us
Humiliare sub potenti manu dei,
The pain it falls in waves across my face
Contremisce et effuge, invocato a
Watch me bleed and start to fall
Nobis sancto et terribili nomine,
The lies they come and twist in pain
Quem inferi tremunt
And then he smiles and calls my name
Ab insidiis diaboli, libera nos, Domine
My knees go weak and I'm here to stay
Ut Ecclesiam tuam secura tibi facias libertate servire
I scream out blood and wash away
Te rogamus, audi nos
His hold on me is deep enough
Ut inimicos sanctae Ecclesiae humiliare digneris
He smiles at my destruction as I wash in fear

Life is but a dream – I make the Earth fall apart
Pithius twists the truth with ribbons of blood
He smells victory in the lies
And coughs blood into the sky

Vade, Satana, inventor et magister
Cross of love burns my skin
Omnis fallaciae, hostis humanae salutis
Let me love and live again
Humiliare sub potenti manu dei,
The truth is covered in sweat and hubris
Contremisce et effuge, invocato a
It wails a song of death exuberent
Nobis sancto et terribili nomine,
And when your tears are dry and spent
Quem inferi tremunt
His teeth gnash and torment you
Ab insidiis diaboli, libera nos, Domine
Where will you run- what will you do?
Ut Ecclesiam tuam secura tibi facias libertate servire
His lies have wings and follow you
Te rogamus, audi nos
His hold on me is deep enough

Ut inimicos sanctae Ecclesiae humiliare digneris
He smiles at my destruction as I wash in fear

The sky's gone out – I make the Earth fall apart
Belial tricks hope free from your hand
As it smashes on the sand
His wicked grimace catches fire

You never know

Dreams Are Just for Dreaming

Why should life go as it should?
Why should happy last forever?
When your dreams flee as you wake
And run from you in terror
Wakeful truth haunts every moment
When you focus on tomorrow
You feel the weakness and the sorrow
Why does hurting last so long?
And sweetness turn so bitter?
The past holds secrets to your future
Barred from the present by condemnation
Situations hold you in your place
And you see life's fleeting moments
Locked in eternal cold suppression
The weight of mistakes slowly crushes you
But not to death – but to life as it is
There are dreams that cannot be
Waking wonder closes opportunity
Closing your eyes won't bring it back
The sleep comes but the dream has fled
Awake or asleep your life is led

By a storm of unpleasant certainty
And you can't touch it or talk to it
Run from it or negotiate
It is what it is whether you leave it or take
And not all storms can be weathered
I had a dream that life would be
Right as rain and good for me
But in the light the morning brings
It doesn't represent what I saw at night
And as I long for the sun to fall
I know I cannot have it all
Or in part
In the day or in the dark

Your Loss or Mine

O sweet dagger – my heart accepts you
With blood and pain you make me mine
As you draw your name in my blood
Each letter deeper into my death
With your face in my eyes I take my last breath
Is your finger cold?
Or has my warmth poured out?
Lay on me until I sleep
Your weight holds me still – keeps me warm
In the agony- my loss torments me
Your caress leads me home
A bloody trail shows the way
But I die before you join me
Only your memory and your mark eternity holds for me
My loss or yours
The world weeps for me
You weep for yourself
And my blood stains your cheek
And you look young again
And I love you each day
As I always have before

All the Cuts They Ache and Burn

Infernal scream he tried to yell
Bracing torment from deepest Hell
Grasping teeth gnashing horrid
Bloody torrent rending morbid

So black his soul – the pitch of night
Fury translates unholy might
The demon twists and turns
And all the cuts they ache and burn

With all my strength but still I crack
I hold his teeth inches from my throat
Bloody plaque and stench so black
Hatred has no antidote

His jagged fangs draw blood
In perfect circles on my neck
I smell the death deep inside
I sense my demise as he opens wide

My blood trickles to his tongue
It lashes sanguine cuneiform
Spells the demon call in tissue on my chest
Tasting agony and ichor in each breathe

I struggle to wake
Fight the bindings on my soul
I thrash about my enemy
Leaking blood I yank and pull

Ancient peril oozing stench
Jaw dislocates agonizing wrench
Jutting closer ever crashing
I feel the warmth from frenzied gnashing

Inhuman strength holding position
Demonic fright crushes disposition
Vomitous pouring languid laughter
Burns my throat passing dark disaster

I pray for day – It doesn't come
I give way fast – not the only one
I can tell others have been eaten
I see their faces tormented pleading

I surrendered to his unholy power
I thought he left me at that hour
But he clenched and the blood poured
His victim whitened on the floor

The Spear of Percival

Searching high for mighty ancestors
Purest concept spawning hate
Coded strength and alabaster
Harder still to contemplate
They rose after mighty death's defeat
Unify at any cost
Shuffle skin and bone to ground
In Satanic holocaust
Deafening hatred built thick walls
Like the coven found at Buchenwald
Totenkopf and broken cross
Foretold the ruin and the loss
Craven leaders forcing will
Easy follow to the kill
Shall be said to come from the Rhine and Hister*
And the demon's name was Adolf Hitler
In search of Holiest Grail
All they founded was Unholy Wail
But he held the Spear of Percival

*Quote from Century 4 Quatrain 68, Michel de
Nostradamus

Vox Demonic: The Prophecy, Quatrains VI-IX

Translation for the Latin in this poem:

Ergo draco maledicte

(Thus cursed demon)

Et omnis legio diabolica

(And every diabolical legion)

Adjuramus te.

(We adjure you)

Cessa decipere humanas creaturas,

(Cease to deceive human creatures)

Eisque aeternae Perditionis venenum propinare.

(And to give to them the poison of eternal Perdition)

_____

_____

Ergo draco maledicte

Clutch your throat as you begin to say

Et omnis legio diabolica

Lies and curses astronomical

Adjuramus te

Pretence or prophecy about that day

Cessa decipere humanas creaturas,

With spewing venom abjure us

Eisque aeternae Perditionis venenum propinare
Unholy prophecies fill the air

Life is but a dream – I make the Earth fall apart
Lyeshy tears open the heart
He speaks in riddle from the middle
Absolute pain and misery word for word

And the demon speaks in its own voice
That of death and decay
And as prophecy it did say:
(The first five quatrains have been lost, those that remain
have been translated from the Russian in which the
demon spoke)

Quatrain VI
В земле орла когда тысячелетие придет люди
заплачут для упования И правда будет сделана
ясно Она была построена на лож и те лож
порождают страх

In the land of the eagle when the millennium comes
The people will cry for hope
And the truth will be made clear
It was built on lies and those lies beget fear

Quatrain VII

Судьба приходит когда крест, котор сгорели гонки
принадлежит и отверганные с презрением другие
Спрошенные начала по мере того как мы вызываем
Черное упование нет упования на всех

Destiny comes when the cross is burned
Some races belong and others spurned
Origins questioned as we call
Black hope isn't hope at all

Quatrain VIII

Объезжая накладные расходы как хищник делают
вспышки смерти пожара в небесном завоевании
Сброс давления как прокалывано в остервенении
Аварии вниз и нищета причин

Circling overhead as the vulture does death
Flashes of fire in heavenly conquest
Collapse as pierced in frenzy
Crashes down and causes misery

Quatrain IX

Шлюха будит от ее сна смерти заново родившийся
по мере того как что-то больше чем она отказывало

прошлый в настоящем моменте Ответствено для
обоих и ее ненависть

The whore awakens from her death sleep
Reborn as something more than she was
Denying the past in the present
Responsible for both as she resents

Ergo draco maledicte
This is what the demon had to say
Et omnis legio diabolica
Truth and curses astronomical
Adjuramus te
Will we out live this day?
Cessa decipere humanas creaturas,
Will the truth burn and then destroy us?
Eisque aeternae Perditionis venenum propinare
Unholy prophecies fill the air

The sky's gone out – I make the Earth fall apart
Muse of misery ignites our fear
We can't pretend we didn't hear
Torment and truth swallow us

You never know

Surrender

Her voice is a blaze across my heart
Piercing intent and travesty
From the end until the start
Never ending maze of confusing colors
Red and blue- the ends of a spectrum
One that only she can see
The hum of a distant echo
Shakes the glass covering my soul
Cracks distort the image
My lover casts on the floor
Through voids in the chamber door
My mind is warmed by her call
Burning with brilliant splendor
Awake and never ending
Is the time until surrender

Mariana Arc

At the bottom of the sea
Just the ocean, you and me
Seafoam forest overhead
Stream is warm but are we dead?
Eerie glow moving slowly
Around your face and hair
Swaying quietly when the wind is missed
Are you a ghost or just not there?
Words in liquid memory
Far too dark for him to see
He longs but alone it seems
She doesn't even know he means
To love her madly at the bottom of the sea
Mariana Arc was her name when she was pretty
When she was living beneath the city
All those long eons before
But she's hot and moves some more
Deeper beneath me and the sea
You can't sense her movement
Her grace and beauty hypnotize
She moves from green to blue before my eyes

Deeper still and more alone
She dances still, but is it with me?
In perfect rhyme and symphony
At the bottom of the sea

Wide Eyed and In Her Wake

She passes when the sun is overhead
No shadow but stirs the air
Eyes flaring like supernova
Hurricane swirling in her hair
Tempestuous fury trails closest
In her wake is apoptosis
Passing wonder and great attractor
Dancing wavelength mimics laughter
What is it that this girl is after?

Often empty contemplation
She mourns the sudden devastation
As she finds her romance lacking
The hounds of hell begin attacking
It isn't her fault she destroys the world
Tidal waves form with just one word
All is well when she's in phase
Once it comes every thirty days
Crashing on us like that tidal wave

She passes more than once each day
Traveling along an ancient way
And if she'll pause her course creation

To dance with me in complication
Laughter oft precedes disaster
The world at her feet- no other place to be
Does she even notice me?
I can't help feeling my mistake
When I'm wide eyed and in her wake

Abyss

Crushing depth around me
Cold runs just as deep
Darkness swirls in misty currents
Autoluminescence gives me hope
Self-absorbed and alone
40,000 feet in four hours
Sudden movement clouds all
Watery cacophony drenches the quiet
In liquid tremors
The fear is tangible when nothing else is
The abyss calls your name
Reaches out to your soul
And presses the life from you in a loving embrace
Wide eyed in your wake
Alone at depth is all I can take
Hold my hand
If you can find your way
It's death in here
And never day

And I See the Demon Face

Time and space
Translocation to this place
Alone and cold
I'm tired and I'm old
When sleep comes upon
I feel weak over strong
I lay to my place
And then I see the demon face
Tight on my chest
Holding my fear
Closely he rests
His fear in my mouth
My heart in his hand
I'm here in my room
But awake in another land

Truth and Beauty

I see truth and beauty
In equal measures
And in that intersection
Words sign the way
To heaven or helplessness
Or both

I feel placid determination
Like the spacing in a constellation
And in that spatial devastation
Latitude overcomes magnitude
To the depths or the shore
Or both

I sense urgency and sorrow
Like wanting more tomorrow
And in that gentle persuasion
Persecution maintains its station
To the front or to the back
Or both

I see truth and beauty
Overlapped and coupled

And in that prosperous union
Urgency seems commonplace
We can now or later
Or both

She Sees Him

Share my thoughts
Hold my hand someday
Come with me
See it all my way
Rest when I call
Sleep as I fall
Pull the world close
When time is short
Even be perverted
Or it might not even hurt
Pulsing love for her smile
If only for a bit
Or even a while
Things like this
Places spin
And it gets thick
Try to run
Or be quick
She sees your heart
Otherwise don't start
Help me see things

By day or by night
In the dark
Or in the light
Slowly the breeze fills the air
Catching her almost unaware
Her smile indicates
She doesn't care
Her hope overrides
When she sees him there

My Luckiest Blue Sweater

Left behind and left for dead
Her words poured wicked through my head
I had it all and I have nothing
She couldn't hold what was just rushing
Maybe if I was smarter
Maybe if I was better
Maybe if I had worn my luckiest blue sweater

I had a hold and let it go
It's all my fault and yes, I know

The last time I saw her she was standing in the dark
She was like estate and I was barely trailer park
She asked me what I wanted
And all I could do was pass
She was in my arms and I couldn't make it last
Maybe if I was smarter
Maybe if I was better
Maybe if I had worn my luckiest blue sweater

I had a hold and let it go
It's all my fault and yes, I know

Beyond her class but she still asks
Why do you stare so hard?
It's all I know, can't let you go
By peering deep I get to keep
Maybe if I was smarter
Maybe if I was better
Maybe if I had worn my luckiest blue sweater

I had a hold and let it go
It's all my fault and yes, I know

Lace and Lyric

She guides the needle with a steady hand
Weaving hope into the fabric of the land
Creating beauty as time passes
This amazing girl is everlasting

Painting landscapes with a word
Mixing context as he should
Landslides and longing here and after
Evaporating all the purest laughter

She pricks her finger in her struggle
Reeling fast far to disaster
The sentence left alone unfinished
By her side to blot the blemish

She weaves a dress and he a rhyme
Destiny calls them in its time
Near at death and wonder's call
She makes him weep as he writes it all

La La Love You

Life and love and satisfaction
Slipping deep with liquefaction
Try to hold and keep it level
The wind and rain speaks about dishevel
Translate while you locate your way

Poor inconvenience by my side
Makes me pale and try to hide
Light of day covered in the dark
Makes it hard to think or remark
Invigorate while you try to escape

Please come over me
When the moon rises to set me free
Pull the joy from overhead
Write all the things I've thought or said
Bifurcate while you contemplate

I've been slow and tired
Troubled and kind of mired
La La Love You carries the day
If I could sing that's what I'd play
Explanation causes consternation

Words and Worlds

Rumination and contemplation
The demon comes to you so slow
Watching what you say and where you go
Seeking weakness and then dive low
Deep into your envy, lust, and pride
Making home and war inside

You won't survive or be alive
When the demon's done with you
He will tear, stretch, and rend
Steal or kill all your friends
And then cut your life in two

If in your fate you find too late
You cannot control this dream
Open your eyes and and fill your lungs
Tear your world apart with your last scream

When the blindness comes
To those around
Close your eyes with them and find the ground

Sleep is cold and then contorted
When your coffin shrinks you get distorted

Words and worlds come to an end

Absolute

You are like the moment before
Water freezes into crystals
The lattice structure starts to set-
Vibrations and oscillations slow
The angles form
And all for one quiet moment is silent beauty
And absolute

I can see worlds in you
And worlds
Worlds in the swirls of your curls
When you shake your head the world turns upside down
And for one small moment
In the fear of destruction
Love is pure

You are like the rain as it wells in the clouds
Misunderstood and admired
Traveling the world falling where you will
Vibrant and needed
Rushing life to those who heeded
In the liquid frenzy
Lust is easy to taste

I can see escape in you
And freedom
Escape and bare excitement in your eyes
When you flutter night and day gives way
And for one small moment
In the fear of whiteout
Dreams are Technicolor

You are like a rainbow before it touches ground
Followed and oft captured
In memory and imagination
Falling to earth with a cacophony
Of wonder and impressive alignment
In the fear of completion
You fall in rhythm

I can see you fall
And as you do I catch you
And set you right
On the earth and under rain drops
Facing the sun
With the moon at your back
And me by your side

Vox Demonic: The Breakpoint

Translation for the Latin in this poem:

Vade, Satana, inventor et magister
(Go away, Satan, inventor and master)
Omnis fallaciae, hostis humanae salutis.
(Of all deceit, enemy of humanity's salvation)
Humiliare sub potenti manu Dei–
(Be humble under the powerful hand of God–)
Exorcizamus te, omnis immundus spiritus
(We exorcise you, every impure spirit)
Omnis satanica potestas, omnis incursio
(Every satanic power, every incursion)
Infernalis adversarii, omnis legio,
(Of the infernal adversary, every legion)
Omnis congregatio et secta diabolica.
(Every congregation and diabolical sect)

_____

—

Vade, Satana, inventor et magister
Leave our hope in tact to laughter
Omnis fallaciae, hostis humanae salutis.

Manic rage you pull right through us
Humiliare sub potenti manu Dei–
Raped and left so demon may I
Exorcizamus te, omnis immundus spiritus
Take the heart but then dare leave us
Omnis satanica potestas, omnis incursio
Blood and spit mark the way for us to go
Infernalis adversarii, omnis legio,
Claw the soul and rend hope to and fro
Omnis congregatio et secta diabolica.
We see the fire burn trust with death sympatico

Life is but a dream – I make the earth fall apart
Astaroth flanked by Aamon and Rashaverak
Crush your spirit and break your back
Hope heats and starts to crack

Vade, Satana, inventor et magister
Death trickles as we stare
Omnis fallaciae, hostis humanae salutis.
Crushing blow and doom provokes us
Humiliare sub potenti manu Dei–
Go white to limp and then you die
Exorcizamus te, omnis immundus spiritus

Gnash the bone while you dissect us
Omnis satanica potestas, omnis incursio
Choked blue with vomit so
Infernalis adversarii, omnis legio,
Hover over calm as we show
Omnis congregatio et secta diabolica.
Crucifix and water sanctimonious

The sky's gone out – I make the earth fall apart
Maxwell's demon heats your soul
Filtering hate and envy in parallel
Then tearing into your heart so well

You never know

Day of Bliss

If you close your eyes for just a moment
A touch of time at darkened perception
Nod of tempestuous petulance
In every direction at once
Seeing nothing
And being seen by all
If you blink you'll miss
Your day of bliss

If you close your mind for just a moment
Perambulation in the nether realm
A glance in the white light of the northern light
Surrounded and singled out
Knowing nothing
And being known by all
If you blink you'll miss
Your day of bliss

If you juxtapose mind and soul for just a moment
Reality turns inside out
You think you exist in the ethereal plane
And you think of God as everything
Becoming love and loved by all

Even blinked
You couldn't miss
We hold and serve your day of bliss

Vox Demonic: The Presence

Translation for the Latin in this poem:

Regna terrae, cantate Deo, psallite Domino
(Kingdoms of Earth, sing to God, praises to the Lord)
Qui fertis super caelum
(That you carry above the sky)
Caeli ad Orientem
(Of heaven to the east)
Ecce dabit voci suae vocem virtutis
(Behold, he sends forth his own voice, the voice of virtue)
Tribuite virtutem Deo.
(Attribute the virtue to God)

Deus caeli, Deus terrae,
(The god of heaven, the god of earth)
Humiliter majestati gloriae tuae supplicamus
(Humbly by the majesty of Your Glory we implore)
Ut ab omni infernalium spirituum potestate,
(That from every power of the infernal spirits)
Laqueo, deceptione et nequitia,
(From their snare, their deception and their wickedness)
Omnis fallaciae, libera nos, Domine.
(Of every deceit, free us, Lord)

Regna terrae, cantate Deo, psallite Domino
Infernal demon within, show yourself so that we may know
Qui fertis super caelum
Swing our way O Demonic Pendulum
Caeli ad Orientem
Bare your shame and show your sin
Ecce dabit voci suae vocem virtutis
Let us hear your voice and so begin to hate us
Tribuite virtutem Deo
The power of Christ rend you to dismissal

Life is but a dream – I make the earth fall apart
Arachula fills the air with the stench of conquest
Demonstrate your hold on life and soul
Give us name and state your hold

Deus caeli, Deus terrae,
Tear through her skin and bare your face in terror
Humiliter majestati gloriae tuae supplicamus
Grow with hate and peer down upon us
Ut ab omni infernalium spirituum potestate,

Fiery blood streaks as we contemplate
Laqueo, deceptione et nequitia,
Appear as power and the spirit of necrosis
Omnis fallaciae, libera nos, Domine.
The ultimate agony for both to pay

The sky's gone out – I make the earth fall apart
Baal hides inside then rips to freedom
Splaying the flesh thus he seeks to impress us
With unholy Power and unholy Presence

You never know

Saint Valentine

Days come and go with faster fluidity
You face the unknown alone
In brief moments you intersect the life of another
Some in passing just a glance
Others with hardly a peer past ignorance
For those few who stop to look at you
Saint Valentine marks the time

Weeks come and go with faster fluidity
You share your fate with o so few
In brief moments you intersect the life of another
Some hardly see your need
Others stop and watch you breathe
For those few who develop love for you
Saint Valentine marks the time

Months come and go with faster fluidity
Emotions play a deeper role in a world with little hope,
full of sorrow
In brief moments you intersect the life of another
Some won't see past tomorrow
Others hold you when you are most weak

For those few who give when they need to take
Saint Valentine marks the time

Years come and go with faster fluidity
The important never fades
In brief moments you intersect he life of another
A small circle of hope and love until the end
If you are one of those
You are my dear friend
And Saint Valentine marks our time

Planetary

She walked the clouds and watched for him
Radiation holding hope aloft as they decay together
Viewing eclipsing moons and longing for his passage
From his world to hers

He swam the liquid torrent and waited for her love
Buoyant desperation keeping his dream afloat
Waves of sorrow wash over him as he peers to the
horizon
Wanting her to come to him

She fears the certain death of taking his gas to her body
But love overcomes her fear
And while she wishes to be near
She journeys forth and sacrifices herself for him

Not seeing his love in the tempest he calls home
He knew her world would crush him
But his love for her demanded he try
And so he went to her world to love her and then die

She struggles to remain afloat in the liquid of his home
She seeks his love with every breath

But finds herself alone
She sinks forever longing for his kiss

He falls along meridian grasping for her love
He seeks another moment to find her in her sky
But explodes from toxic sorrow
And without her love he dies

Levitate Me

Can't you see the effect you have on me?
Twists and turns but with you the road is straight
The clock ticks but the time is never late
Won't you watch the moon with me?

Grasping for Luna and your hand
All around the world stops
And notices the smile on your face
The darkside seems brighter now

Levitate Me
High above reality
Float me to the place where my dreams
All come true
Levitate Me

Don't you feel the effect you have on me?
Shakes and shivers but not from the cold
The water drips but we are never wet
Won't you watch the moon with me?

Grasping Luna and your hand
The universe pauses its' dance

And bows low before you – a stellar genuflection
Hungers for your affection

Levitate Me
High above reality
Float me to the place where my dreams
All come true
Levitate Me

Don't you fathom the depths of my devotion?
Mariana is not deep or wide enough to hold it all
The wind blows but we are never dry
Won't you watch the moon with me?

Grasping Luna and your hand
Time stands by to watch you sleep
Your body is warm and the world is cold
The mix makes the planets stir
And all the while I pine for you

Levitate Me
High above reality
Float me to the place where my dreams
All come true
Levitate Me

Blue

Blue and the smell of wild flowers
White on the waves and the sun overhead
Can this be, for someone like me, a reality?
Then you realize you are dead

Lilacs and rose petals in your hair
Tangerine dreams and a sweet tomorrow
Can this wonder be for me?
Until you remember the sorrow

Archaic splendor and gilded terraces
Smiles for miles and glad you're here
It all seems so wonderful
There's a quake and then the fear

You're all shattered and it all mattered
Then there was just blue and what's left of you

Vox Demonic: Requiem

Translation for the Latin in this poem:

Requiem æternam dona eis, Domine
(Eternal rest grant unto them, O Lord)
Et lux perpetua luceat eis
(And let perpetual light shine upon them)
Ab omni vinculo delictorum
(From all the chains of their sins)
Libera animas omnium fidelium defunctorum
(Free the souls of all the faithful departed)
De pœnis inferni et de profundo lacu
(From infernal punishment and the deep pit)

Requiem æternam dona eis, Domine
Show evil and perdition the only Way
Et lux perpetua luceat eis
Rise above unholy rancor by standing on the marble dais
Ab omni vinculo delictorum
With heavy chains and fetters abhor them
Libera animas omnium fidelium defunctorum
From utter void and beyond decorum

De pœnis inferni et de profundo lacu
The Unholy Beast torments to distract you

Life is but a dream – I make the Earth fall apart
LaPlace's Daemon also knows my heart
He traces with Newton the courses of your action
Infernal torment leads to utter destruction

Requiem æternam dona eis, Domine
Set me apart for sacrifice this day
Et lux perpetua luceat eis
Dismember in abyss and scream to please us
Ab omni vinculo delictorum
Lash my wrists with burnt hair and score them
Libera animas omnium fidelium defunctorum
Leave me broken and bled at sanctum sanctorum
De pœnis inferni et de profundo lacu
Look in my eyes and make me hate you

The sky's gone out – I make the Earth fall apart
Descarte's Daemon causes doubt
He fills the water with worms and vomit
Fire and ice issue from the comet

You never know

Cut the Skin

Cut the skin and then begin
To give red lust a chance
Cut the skin again, again
Blood trailing oft unholy dance
Cut the skin when I say when
Follow closely horrid romance
Cut the skin until you're in
Change to hollow from a hopeful stance
Cut the skin while seeking men
Deviated terror during your trance
Cut the skin cut the skin
When I say when
When I say when

mighty flash and ever last

mighty flash and ever last
the righteous have just fallen
the spinning stopped as it began
here is a vortex for us to fall in
we scream we kick we gnaw we gnash
we contemplate a never ending spiral
we bite our tongue and spit out blood
the bitter taste of sanguine going viral

St. Ann the Tormentor

Betwixt and between
The moments I have as a free man
Is a flurry of beauty and eternal grace
From my tormentor Saint Ann

I lay still in bed at night
Silent while awake
I see Saint Ann's shadow over me
My soul is hers and hers alone to take

My eyes sense her over me
Hands splayed across my chest
I yield to her in mind and deed
Though she hesitates to let me rest

I hardly surrender in my dreams
But she does what she can
It's hard to fight against the fear
Emanating from Saint Ann

Blood and tears streak my face
I cry against the precepts of a man
The world seems dark and strange
When tormented by sweet Saint Ann

Saint Ann is not alone when she torments me
Dragons flash by in the twilight
Her sword arcs overhead
Claws scratch the earth as they take flight

She severs my soul from me in one cruel stroke
And I cry out with remembrance of past pleasures
There is no blood on her gown
But there is blood in her eyes

If I could change my fate by action
And rearrange my eternal plan
I'd not shield or hide my soul
From my tormentor Saint Ann

She is Mine

I saw her from afar that day
And I was clearly taken
She was an angel set free on us
As we were not forsaken

I sent her flowers and poetry
My longing transcending passion
She smiled while singing in the sun
And was aloof as was her fashion

My fire burned much brighter now
I just had to possess her
She danced by the moonlight then
And responded to my love with laughter

I wrote of my deep love for her
My ache collapsed in a crash of thunder
She barely saw the words I wrote
Eyes burning through the page in wonder

I called to the gods to save me
I begged them help me if they can
I received a flash of clarity
And in it perceived a plan

My struggle has come to an end
All my fears are laid to rest
I have her heart after all this time
And I keep it on my desk

The End

Seasons change or remain the same
We are here and then departed
Reflections seem more real than truth
And the end it seems has started

Unforgiving but go on living
The past trails far behind
The hurt has come and then it's gone
Let it flee far from your mind

Another day another year
Troubles high and low
The patience of your virtue dear
Doesn't seem to want to know

When it goes away you see
It will be like losing a friend
For bitter tastes the wind you see
When it portends the end

The Kraken and St. John Cassian

The maelstrom swirled around us now
The water tended to blacken
The shriek of wind and crash of wave
Heralded the coming of the kraken

The black eyes of the beast
Offer deep demise to those who see
A longing glance as you stared
While others tried to flee

The vilest of communication passes
From dark and ancient origin
The priest rides the water dragon
Venom spewing as the basest sin

Eight claws clutch as doom
Ever placing you in squalor
Sucking the flesh from your bones
And burning away your valor

Eight paths to deepest hell
The river bridged anon
The gates open widely for you
Your passage has been won

If you desire all in excess
Smother food with wildest honey
The kraken pulls you close to him
Your sin has the taste of gluttony

If you are weakest in the flesh
And given into cold temptation
The kraken pulls you close to him
As you kiss the lips of fornication

If you want to take what others have
Above a desire to be seen as righteous
The kraken pulls you close to him
Because you smell of covetous

If you hate with deepest pain
Because of strongest languor
The kraken pulls you close to him
Your sin is bloody anger

If your lack of confidence
Leeds to feelings of rejection
The kraken pulls you close to him
For you suffer from dejection

If burdened by a troubled heart
And possessing a demonic malady
The kraken pulls you close to him
You are weak from weariness and accidie

If a lust for self above all others
Tells the sad but truest story
The kraken pulls you close to him
He senses pride and vainest glory

If truest love you contemplate
Has no base in common happenstance
The kraken pulls you close to him
Your sin is willful arrogance

Many ways to find your end
While dancing with the dragon
At least we have a warning tale
Told to us by a saint called Cassian

Perfect Progress

Look now how she has grown
She draws them with her smile
The Princess never sleeps it seems
But maybe after while

Her look tells tales of long before
When she was just a girl
With satin ribbons in her hair
That would glimmer when she'd twirl

Amazed wonder as she turns
To talk or play some childhood game
She seems a little different now
But in many ways the same

Her spirit rose to meet the day
She makes her own decisions
And even though not nearly perfect
She is the subject of no derision

A look above her age it seemed
To carry her far away
She fled from Mediocrity
And doesn't live near there this day

Her brightness fills the space around
The area where she dwells
She has exceeded every possibility
And her kindness comes in swells

The pieces of her heart return
Never again to go
She holds them all together now
With not a single foe

Freedom was all she needed
Far from expectation
To become the girl that God had made
A wondrous revelation

I see a perfect girl today
That's how this story goes
Perfect thought, perfect deed
Perfect word, perfect prose

Missy Aggravation IV

Splashing in the fountain
Rinsing away perspiration
Water from our private mountain
Missy Aggravation

Holding hands in the dark
The warmest affiliation
Walking slowly to the park
Missy Aggravation

Decays for days
All of her own radiation
She's in all my plays
Missy Aggravation

Heavens cast a purple glow
She's divine illumination
I watch her dance to and fro
Missy Aggravation

There she was in the snow
Preternatural realization
I stopped cold too watch her go
Missy Aggravation

Everything and Nothing

Feelings of joy follow closely behind the King
Never at his side but several paces back
In reach but never in his grasp
What must it be like to have everything and nothing?
One knows and knows when to pretend
It is all beginning but also at an end

Swim currently strong and let go
Don't hold on for long
Not yours to grasp it's in the past
What must it be like to let go when you want to hold on?
One sees and knows when not to
It seems so far but it's also close to you

Offered what was his alone
Broken on the offering stone
Held his hand against some will
Dropped the blade before the kill
What must it be like to kill when you want life?
Talked it down and walked it off
Had it all and had enough

Rammed his way past that day
Survival poured from the cloud
All was quiet and then got loud
What must it be like to hear when there is no sound?
All seemed lost
And then was found

Nimrod's son called that great day
Another solar agitate
It all came fast and tried to sway
What must it be like to go when you want to stay?
It died inside slowly at first
It all got quiet before it burst

Sisters of a Sort

The complex mind wanders far sometime
The river flows and there it goes next to a friend of mine
Her name is Charity and she sees rainbows from afar
The colors run together she can see each one
They all look the same in the brightness of the sun
So each day is grey even though at night it all looks white
Charity Sometimes sleeps next to Melody
In the same house but in different rooms
Or are they closer? Seems at most it would be simple
To tell when one came and the other went
In between is heaven sent and there it also went
I saved saved saved and then I spent
What did I get but the river flowing close
With rainbows on each end and a letter from a friend
Quite a conflagaration Melody, Charity, and Missy
Aggravation

Rebirth to War

Cross laced and ridden
Dropped far and hidden
The depths become dark as pitch
There were lights before but they are no more
My eyes focus on strange sights
I see demons battling golden knights
Great battles and blood running
Shrieks of hate come from every direction
I turn to flee and a demon waits for me
Comets crash the lava flows
I saw hope but there it goes
Doom tastes as ash on my tongue
I swallow and tomorrow comes
The dagger draws – my blood on the blade
I cut the earth my own grave
Cold and old the spirit fades
The roar continues to hold the earth
I'll see it more on my rebirth

Missy Aggravation III

She has a cutting affection
There will be no mutilation
Points it all in my direction
Missy Aggravation

She looks like a meteorite
Defying all computation
Traveling out of sight
Missy Aggravation

Purely hypothetical
Responsible for devastation
The opposite of heretical
Missy Aggravation

Erie feelings of longing
Equivalent to forestation
Part of me wants belonging
Missy Aggravation

Deepest regard I know it's hard
Planetary manipulation
She eludes all but regard
Missy Aggravation

Missy Aggravation II

I walked in from long ago
She sees me with trepidation
We'll put on quite a show
Missy Aggravation

There is a story here
There is no correlation
Not lost in fear
Missy Aggravation

Fractions seem whole
Her smile is constellation
I can feel her pull
Missy Aggravation

Separate but equal
We should be compilation
There must be a sequel
Missy Aggravation

She has a fair complexion
Mistress of the reformation
Me the written rhythm section
Missy Aggravation

Missy Aggravation

I had a dream about a girl
Curls and a look like confirmation
There she is on my TV
Missy Aggravation

She gives her time
I listen to her radio station
And I give her mine
Missy Aggravation

I give her rhyme
I take her when I vacation
And she takes her time
Missy Aggravation

A smile on my face
In quiet contemplation
When she reads this
Missy Aggravation

INTENTIONALLY FLAWED

My eyes are green
Or maybe brown
My soul is frayed or is it clawed
From top to bottom
I'm intentionally flawed

Intention you draw and wonder at the flaw
It's not my intention you see
But the gods above me
What can I do but know it
And try not to flee

Words can come quickly
Too quick for thought
It's a curse and a destination- really
But it's what I've got
'Cause I'm intentionally flawed

The truth is often difficult to swallow
And others paths are hard to follow
So I'll go my own way- at least today
I'll get started when the chill has thawed
I'm a slow starter- I'm intentionally flawed

If I stay up late my mind starts to wander
In quiet contemplation and often consternation I explore
Here and now and so much more
I compile a list with troubled awe
It's long and contains my every flaw

Deep seeded fear of ignorance
Despite the presence of intelligence
If only the end were heaven sent
I'd leave now but I've paid some rent
Haven't you heard? I'm intentionally flawed

I've gotten speed and fallen down
My feet don't often tough the ground
But wait— when no one else is around
Do you think you hear that sound?
It's the recitation of my sins
It doesn't start and it never ends

I'm intentionally flawed
And so are you...
What will you do?

You are Not Ordinary

Melody Sometimes
A construct of subterfuge
Remembering her effervescence
From the past and in the present
You are many things I'm told
I cannot know because you are not mine
I believe them though
I remember when
We kissed and it was all true then
And it's all true now
I remember how
You made me smile even though
It's been a while
Comprehensive good and ever knowing
Love and kindness overflowing
Knowing when to stop and when to go
Your aren't mine
But these things I know
Melody Sometimes
A construct of subterfuge

But good none the less
In white lace and blue dress

All Gone Cold

The fire burns bright
And her hold on me is tight
The flames pull me in fast
And she peers into me again
Yellow and red the flames flicker
Debriefing another extroverted candidate
One ember at a time
No reason and no rhyme required
Their time has expired
She moves and I watch
Too hot to touch
The flames pull me in fast
And it won't last for long
Her will is too strong
Debilitating laugh across the night sky
The embers die
And it has all gone cold

She Smells Different

Fragrance is what she left me
When she walked away the other day
I asked- no begged – for her to stay
Subtle smile but not my way
Better she left anyway
Now I smell the way she was
And it's better than the way she is
Ironic isn't it? But we should quit
She will hear us and tremble
Ire full force and terrible
Splendid anger leveled quietly
Building force and frustration
Spotting us above our station
Leading to dreadful demonstration
And the fragrance will go away
Sucked from the room by her void
Cold and hard – devastating
So I'm still waiting
For that girl I used to know
The fragrance will tell me so
When she smells like she is

Like I used to know
Remember when she had to go?

Failed and Full of Holes

Exasperated and perforated
Failed and full of holes
The life wasn't what it seemed it would be
Love and anger flee from me
I'm left with sorrow and no tomorrow
Would you smile about that?
Well I can't and can't understand how you could
Maybe you don't really live here
Area 51's daughter leading me to the slaughter
Explains and at greats pains
Silver glow and there you go
I'm failed and full of holes

Into a Shady Place

If I fell from the sky forever
I'd want to land in a shady place
But it would never come
So I'd think it about as I tumbled
Through the sky and wonder why
I would never see it

The sky would be so cold
The air around me warm
I'd fall faster and into the swarm
The buzzing cacophony of wonder
As I fell I'd call your name
Would you hear me, would I sound the same?

If I fell from the sky forever
I'd think about the time I spent
Complaining about life on solid ground
And I'd look around
And see it wasn't so terrible after all
But still I fall

I'd want to land in a shady place
Where the sun wouldn't find me

The coolness would calm my soul
But I don't know
I'm falling from the sky forever
So I will never see it

If Tomorrow Never Came

Why don't we
Take tomorrow by the hand
Lead it far outside the plan
Travel to another land
Where things haven't yet began
And try it all again – try it all again

My head was feeling scared but my heart was feeling free

Hope for a new tomorrow
Where things aren't begged or borrowed
Hold each other as we go
Living far away from the show
It's all possible didn't you know
And try it all again – try it all again

My head was feeling scared but my heart was feeling free

Can't you leave it all behind
And then run away with me
We'd go all the way you'd see
So far that we could be free

If you'd only go with me
And try it all again – try it all again

My head was feeling scared but my heart was feeling free

Why don't we
Take today and throw it all away
So that we can go and play
For even just one day
Girl, what do you say?
Try it all again? Try it all again?

My head was feeling scared but my heart was feeling free
Would you come and go with me?
Would you come and go with me?

Crystal Chrysanthemums

Frozen rain numbs the pain
Of another brush with happiness
But as the ice melts it waters the field
Where the wild flowers bloom
In multi-color splendor
And happiness seems closer than before
The blues, reds, and yellows
Make my tears dry on my cheek
And I yearn for someone to watch with me
That dream remains lost in time
But the crystal chrysanthemums are mine

Tradition as Trespass

We moved to the new neighborhood
And were welcomed by many
The house was already built and lived in
For thousands of years it seemed
Our closest friends were from Babylon, Persia, Greece,
and Rome
The tapestry was rich with historic revelation
Their eyes seemed ancient and full of truth
They were here before and they knew it
Those here before were their kin
Were even still friends with them
With knowing glances they told us so
They smiled at our pretence
Our name on the door did nothing to change the fact
That we were trespassing on ancient ground
For it was not our house at all
We just stole the space for our own
Everyone seemed to know but us
We protested our claim
We fabricated stories and meanings
And some believed

But that changed nothing

We were trespassing

And recent fiction now called tradition

Cannot change history at all

Tears Like Honey

Everything she is seems supernatural
The way she moves at times is ethereal
Her words sound as falling rain
As it strikes the water's surface
Soothing and comforting
As she utters syllables of peace and remembrance
Her smile radiates magnificence
Central to the theme of her perfection
All the birds fly in her direction
Called by the beauty of her countenance
And the fragrance of her hair
We all watch as she moves by
The wind and seas by her side
Lost among the brilliance of her soul
Pale as the moon before the sun
Darkened by the shadow of longing
She smiles at me and in that gentle glow
I see tears on her ruby cheeks
As I kiss them gently away
I know what no other may
Her Tears Taste Like Honey

The Dialectic

The air feels hot and then cold
And I feel young while I'm still old
I somehow start and suddenly stop
I'm at the bottom and then at the top

I say yes when I mean no
I want to stay but try to go
I look high when I should look low
And I move fast when I should move slow

I pretend knowledge when I don't know
I move to when it should be fro
I try to run when I should walk
I quietly listen but instead should talk

I think ugly but appear beautiful
I try rebellion when I should be dutiful
I speak when I don't know a thing to say to you
I color the world red when clearly it's blue

I walk and go no place
I tend to collapse when I need more space
I try to see tomorrow when I need to see today
I want to work when I should play

Things seem great when they are small
Life seems complete but that's not all
I try to hold it when it should fall
I move in timidity when I should be tall

I protect when I could break
I see mountains and then a lake
I give when I should keep
And I lay awake when I should sleep

Will You Do It If I Ask You?

Frenzied gnashing so distracting
Pulsing fear is getting near
It's hard for me to scream with worry
When I can't see and I can't hear
Don't kill me fast – there is no hurry
Make it hurt until I'm buried

Will you do it if I ask you?

Dread and glory so distracting
As you destroy I beg for more
You leave a scar across my face
I can't see who I was before
Magnify your hate and fill this place
Please don't slow but keep your pace

Will you do it if I ask you?

The World Revolves for Ruby

Ruby sees all that she can see
And the world belongs to her
It spins to keep her warm
And tilts to catch her fancy
The rain washes her hair
And the wind dries her curls
The sand covers her steps
To protect her from man
With Ruby the world is right again

Ruby dances when the birds sing
And sleeps when the moon lights the night
The trees offer shade
And Ruby sings to them in gratitude
The stars dance for Ruby and make her smile
The rainbow leads Ruby to happiness
And she is safe along its course
Guarded from envy and man
With Ruby the world is right again

Liquid Amber

Liquid amber and the splendor it possesses
Reminds me of changes in us all
Fading from green to red
And the coming of a golden age
Graced with the beauty from the start
Revealed as Invictus comes and goes
Leaving the past wind swept
The blend of color excites the mind
Wondrous pleasure comes in new colors
With the eternal passing of time
Autumn leads us to a new place
Where the kiss of the sun is gone
But you still feel warm inside
The water freezes at the surface
But you can remember the ripples that will come again
And they are mimicked as a smile on your lips
A kiss brings warmth and the air doesn't seem so cold
Fall is the time to be held and to hold
White over yellows and reds
The leaves are covered in snow
The wind exposes the rainbow beneath

When it decides to
Nature takes its toll
And it is a price we gladly pay

The Sun Will Set for You

When the trees have no leaves
And the stars are quiet in the sky
What exactly will you do?
Will the sun set for you?

When the water is still
And the whispers of the wind fill your mind
What exactly will you do?
Will the sun set for you?

When the people around you cease to move
And phosphorescent flutters fill the air
What exactly will you do?
Will the sun set for you?

When time rolls along
And you sing a different song
What exactly will you do?
Will the sun set for you?

When the sun demands justice
And the tides all rise
What exactly will you do?
Will the sun set for you?

When the universe calls
And your will expands
What exactly will you do?
Will the sun set for you?

When the fear runs away
And the moon comes out to play
What exactly will you do?
Will the sun set for you?

If I decided
What the sun would do
Then I would make
The Sun Set for You

Sorrow

I tried to erase the memories
Of days with you and days with me
Something holds on when the will is gone
And the memories linger on

Be strong and don't cry
Even if you have a reason
Hold your breath and carry on
There'll be another season

Fret if you can
Alone and with the lights off
Don't push your sorrow under the door
It has a key anyway

Change your address
If that will help you sleep
It won't matter much
Sorrow knows where you live

Try to sleep when it all fades
I know you can't
The trembling comes
And the fear too in waves

Rest well and contemplate
Insurrection of the will
Another name for fate
Passion does not cross that line

Me? I don't sleep anyway...

The Train

Be careful what you ask for
Someone who cares might offer
To make it so and right
And therefore all the time becomes as night
And the birds land softly near

The train carries all it can
Up the world and down again
It doesn't slow around the bend
So please step back – be safe my friend
Toss your worry in the bin
Let the train carry your sin
And off it goes and up again
Called by another seekers whim

The sound of the train
Drives away the birds
The day breaks through the night
And all seems right
Toss your worry in the bin
The train has come around again
It doesn't cause me any refrain
We all need a friend and a train

When She Walks

Every day at noon
She passes by my room
My mind watches while my eyes stay aloof
She sees my thoughts
And knows my eyes are lonely
Maybe she walks slower than she should?

If this were my own dream
I'd walk beside her and listen to her breath
I'd comfort as I could
While matching her steps with my own
She sees me in her shadow
Maybe she moves closer than she should?

The clouds move and her shadow disappears
I look to see the manifestation above
Some malicious god offends me deep
My ire grows and her steps seem faint
My concern has driven her from me
Maybe she loved when she should have not?

Endless Pain for A Walk in the Rain

Liquid memories overhead
Staining white linen bloody red
The dragon's eyes wander far
Reflections of death and carnival

Intrepid flight and deepest vision
Soaring thoughts held to derision
Darkest fog forms indecision
All along to hold the mission

Nestled quietly in complication
She holds aloft in highest station
Peering intently into darkness
Seeking blackest aberration

I'm sick he cried as she fell of the ladder
The dragon circled
To see what's the matter

Weakness and terror fill the room
The pain of impact
Is in full bloom

The claws explain all
And the madness grows
All was lost due to the fall

From the cradle to the grave
It is but an increment to obtain
But welcome harbor
From life's falls and all the pain

Her gaze causes men to go insane
And hide their hope
From all their pain
To live is loss and loss again

You are the only love I've ever had
Red and white in a lover's plaid
Losing you makes me so sad
Why does it all have to feel so bad?

The dragon's eyes find all it needs
The fall it seems planted hateful seeds
Aloft and pressing ever near
All around he feels her fear

She claims him fast as she
Tears out the past and he

Won't last long for
A heart is an inconsolable void

Desolation
Consternation
Condemnation
Aberration

How can he hide from all the pain?
What can he think to not go insane?
When can he live to live once again?
Maybe he should take A Walk in the Rain

Liquid memories overhead
Staining white linen bloody red
The dragon's eyes wander far
Reflections of death and carnival

Nevermind

Across oceans of time on a buoy of hope
With ink etched in dried fiber
Drops of salt water run the words together
But memory holds the meaning well

The sun beats down and dries the words
As the paper is held aloft
Preserved through wash and wave
If twisted just a bit

Long days drive wild thoughts
But those first words burn deep
And as night comes he dreams of those days
Before the storm roiled beneath

He sees her before him, sometimes looking away
In wondered thoughts of yore
Confidence shows in her eyes
As if she wants something to explore

She begs her past for redress from the challenge that lay
ahead
But he peers intently past her fears

Gives her hope to grasp instead
And she slowly smiles as if accepting generosity

Days seem like ages
Civilizations arise, crescendo, and then fall
Their sorrow is drowned out and out
By another sirens call

Unwelcome disposition came, alone again
He finds himself afloat
Held up by regret and indecision
He writes to her a note

When we meet again, these words I will speak to you:
I should have left behind the past
Composed and matured anon
Focused just on you alone
And let us carry on

The clouds came quickly overhead
As if driven on the run
The wind blew fiercely from the east
While rain blotted out the sun

The flood was infinitely quiet
As it swept me out to sea

The need to see you once again
Was the buoy that came to me

I swallowed water and tears
My fate seemed assured
But clutch the words I held so dear
Was my final act of courage

I said I'd tell you everything
If God only spared my life
And then the nighttime loneliness
Took me down again and claimed my present life

Time passed as did the water underneath
Left my sorrow far behind
I had seen the world from perspective high
The memories deep within my mind

There she was, from long ago
A new flood caught me from behind
My balance lost, I tumbled to ground
And memories filled my mind

I grasped for the paper and words contained
An olde promise to fulfill

Our eyes matched and thoughts aligned
And it was enough, so Nevermind.

Hyacinth

Thoughts of her provoking sleep
Then eyes wide open
She passes by in her corridor
And I lean in hope of contact

She is sheathed by the sun
Glossy and out of reach
Her smile warms the air
Her beauty breaks the peace

I pretend she knows me
And my solitude slips in this fiction
Pleasant as it is
Time is not on my side

She is a hyacinth girl
And she rides the breeze to sea
And back as a mist on us all
Cooling as she passes

Memories don't fade
Her vibrance drives away the haze
And memories flood over the years
And today starts to fade into yesterday

She's a lioness this day
As she passes my way
She peers into mine
And there stops the time

Green Eyes

Green eyes—windows to the soul—surrounded by
Black hair—a beautiful flow— framing
A warm smile—inviting me close—drawing me in
So much for me to know

What could be dreamt in a dream?
Would she be like you?
I don't have to wait and wonder
I see you and I know—reality is better than fiction

How did we get to this point?
I am so hard to know—but you know me so well
And now I hold you so dear
You found a way in—and I hope you stay
I'm trying to see all the brightness of your colors—and
You are fantastic by night and day

The Sweetest Thing is the draw that comes unannounced
Why did we meet? How did we find each other?
It was supposed to be—an intersection of you with me
You cause me to search for words, but
There is always some way to make a silence be spoken

Overwhelmed by you—my heart beats inspired
And the cores of our being must meet
And overlap as intended
So I will dream the possibilities when I can't be with you

I have but one true love I know
She sings to me—in my solitude
And I know her name—and she knows mine
I try to know her in all her changes

When we are together we forget about ourselves and
think of the other
I start to melt when your eyes turn my way
And I start to melt—when your mind turns my way
And it's all I can do not to faint

Your beauty is my strength—and my weakness
The beauty of your heart, mind, and the shadow that you
cast
Shields me from the sun
And lets me glow in your light
As it was meant to be

Brown eyes—mine this time—looking onto yours
Brown hair—framing my smile

Matching yours—inviting you close—drawing you in
So much for you to know

A beautiful dream
You are the sweetest thing
Inspired
I will dream true love
She sings to me—and it's all I can do not to faint
Your beauty lets me glow
Drawing you in
So much for you to know

Dawn

Dawn sees the sun break through sullen darkness and stir
the birds
Who fly with memories of actions past and mistakes in
their talons
Deeds done before his love that were not meant to be or
meant to last
She sees my eyes pierce past and present when I look her
way
Gazing on her face with love although it's only days
Complete affection for her shows all others in the midst
Water breaks upon the sands and she whispers to him
this:
"I love you too, Dear"
Birds swoop and pick at fruit left on the branches nearby
Fruit grown in place for another so sweet to have
Who can tell the ripe from the rest?
Or the chaff from the wheat? Or the easy from the best?
Together fast and hopeful, loving past all others
Hold my hand and walk with me for an age and another
I promise we won't leave tracks for others to follow
Or get lost along the way

Commit to me your love and affection for uncertain is the day
I'll protect your heart, and our walk will be long
Sitting side by side to see the beauty of the Dawn

Since I Met You

Touch the surface of a comet
Longing lost trajectory
Passing nimbly effervescent
Mixing all of you with me

Perfect drop of falling water
Splashing ideal symmetry
Prism of romantic splendor
Mixing all of you with me

Ray of light falling quickly
Heavenly and planetary
From the sun into your eyes
Mixing all of you with me

Feel the movement of the ocean
Next to me and by the sea
Holding on to both my hands
Mixing all of you with me

Quickly coming moving slowly
Subtle blur and hard to see
Kissing sends the joy of heaven
Mixing all of you with me

Our eyes meet in fearful wonder
You move your body next to mine
Synthesis of pleasure pounding
As you're mixed with me this time

Needful Things

She opens up her mind and heart
And pours out needful things
Feeling for someone who hears
And understands the same

Hurt from others less than her
No match for what she gives
Dishonest as they played the game
And lied right where she lives

Passive is her love to give
Because others have taken
She is slow to give again
As others have forsaken

A new person meets her anon
And listens to her woes
He understands her pain and sorrow
And knows just how it goes

He honors her request for patience
And he gives it to her freely heeded
Loving all he sees with her
He'll be just what she needed

Special though they hardly know
The things that will pass between them
Every time he hears her voice
He hopes that she will need him

Terrible Insight

Deep understanding of iambic pentameter
Rhythm and rhyme and perfect composure
Covered in moonlight avoiding exposure
Treasured word buried deep in lore

Seeking some semblance of normality
Venturing utterance quietly
Eyes peering to discover
One more aspect and then another

She watches and she knows
Her memory fills with wisdom and worry
Her lips move with cold and then intent
She seeks to speak and hurry

She talks of the things best heard at night
When wrong has a hold over reason and right
All things shake with the fever of fright
And truth has nary a place to alight

Comfort pours over you
But you feel tired from its weight

The Nymph and the Honeybee

The flutter of wings tell a tale if you listen
Of natural collaboration and sweat that glistens
On the wings of the humble, hardworking honeybee
Flowers give what they must while the honeybee gently takes
Together yielding nectar after while
The sweetest way to make a smile

Struggle, sorrow, victory, and celebration
Flowers feel her touch with anticipation
The world is sweeter when two worlds collide
Time passes and the sun moves overhead
Honeybee, what do you see?

She walks and the flowers turn her way
Her melody causes trees to sway
Her smile lights the fields and brings the day
Honeybee, what do you see?

Together in the field watching exuberant life
Alighted on her hand, the honeybee warmed by her breath
Honeybee, what do you see?

Melodic dance and symphony
Beautiful Nymph and Honeybee

Honeybee, what do you see?

The Cupboard is Empty

A drastic grasp at the inevitable

Leaves you holding the obvious

And you close your eyes and cherish

Unable to protract or reflect

Now means all that it can

And the cupboard is empty

The curtains move in the breeze

And the water pours over cracked tile

The storm has entered the house

Lightning charges the air

Eyes wide in wonder with each flash

And the cupboard is empty

Quiet steps move closer to freedom

The doors creep open slowly

The sound almost loud enough to be heard

Wicked claps of thunder shred any peace

Fear fills the room with each moment

And the cupboard is empty

Holding dread at bay with effort

Comfort doesn't come to you

The wind moves your hair

And you don't care

The whispers come faster now

Unable to breath or turn you notice

The cupboard is empty

Memories race through corridors in your mind

Each turn slows remembrance

Time is short and it all fades

The doors slowly close as you approach

The cupboard is empty

But it once held hope in rows

Death Won't Come Quickly

(My son's favorite)

Not quite there
My eyelids frozen
Scared awake by the path I've chosen
Cold steel gleaming in my hand
Wet with blood and fear again

The world passes slowly beneath my feet
Death won't come quickly this way

Almost content
With passing fancy
In my hand the cup of poison
A long drink and my lips are moistened

Almost awake
Breaths collapsing quickly
Hands choke her white
She's pale and sickly
Destruction possessed by my fingers
Crushing grip intent to linger

The world passes slowly beneath my feet
Death won't come quickly this way

Almost content
The fantasy smolders
All the while
My heart grows colder

Eyes wide open
Anger growing
Rope pulls tightly
Breathing slowing
She dies silent and alone
Her pain was ended long ago

The world passes slowly beneath my feet
Death won't come quickly this way

Almost content
I'm cold and older
The fire in my eyes
No longer smolders

Lucidity is now my friend
She's by my side
The killings end
Wide awake and hate departed

Too bad it's come
After the killing started

The world passes slowly beneath my feet
Death won't come quickly this way

Wisps

Wisps of her hair frame her face
But his love for her has no bounds
He watches the sparkles in her eyes
And he counts each one in turn
They represent the reasons he loves her
He touches her face and sees the world anew
His perspective changed by the feelings she evokes

She responds to his wonder and reaches for his hands
Her touch brings him to the day they met
When his heart was filled for the first time

He passed by her and stopped at once
Her beauty took his paceAnd in its' place
He was struck with awe and amazement
He had not the courage or the words
But he had to hear her voice

I would like to know your name
And spend my time with you
As you pass into this realm
Just tell me what to do

It was true love expressed
His being consumed by hope
He waited for her to come to him
He anticipated her beauty like the rising of the sun
She was his Sunshine

He captured his feelings as words
Of love and care for her
He placed his prose into her care
And hoped for love returned

She filled his heart with hope and wonder
And her touches brought him joy

She was beside him now- walking with him
Hand in hand
Heart to heart
And would always be by his side
Yesterday, Today and Tomorrow

He looked over to her and noticed a strand of hair across
her face
He pulled her close to him and kissed her gently
And moved the hair behind her ear, kissing her again
This time with passionate abandon

Her face was framed again as on the day they met
When she stopped him in his place

Sunshine and Sorrow were never friends
His heart was filled with one
And forever free of the other

You are a Drug

Magic movements across a tablet
Passion unconfined to words or actions
Lusty forces pull to completion
Exuberant and complete satisfactions

Actions quickly finding mark
With eyes wide open in the dark
Her voice pours over me like water on smooth rocks
I melt for her when I hear her talk

Culmination resounding with echoes of passion
Surrounding me with loves distraction
Exposing want and desire so pleasing
With word of mouth aptly teasing

Final manipulation and demonstration
Expulsion of victory and passion
Fire ignited and burning bright
Cradling affection through the night

You are the reason for late nights and sleepless wonder
Times of want and unsatisfied hunger
Rolling thoughts eternally tug
All the time– you are a drug

Sixty Percent

Reckoning our time together
From every day to just whenever
I had hoped for all the time
To be with you and keep you mine

Change has come to make me pay
Losing time with you today
I didn't know just what to say
But you said we'd be okay

Made forlorn with want and sorrow
Because there is no you tomorrow
Is there another time to borrow?
So I'm not lost alone and harrowed

Door Opens Slowly

The door opens slowly, creaking as it has for years.
The light from the hall makes me squint
But I can see a figure moving clearly near.

I hold your gaze as I step from the light,
Following you always into the night
As your lashes narrow and hold my stare,
I hear you whisper, "Are you really there?"

Hope blossoms in my pounding heart
Floor boards silent under bare feet
The glow behind engulfs you in sparks of light
As you say, "I am here. And yours tonight."

Twin peridots glimmer and my emotions grow
As if to realize a self I didn't quite know.
I search the dark to find you, my key.
I want to understand that spark you put in me.

Embracing you as for the first time
Loving you— for you are mine
We are complete—you and me
Being together is the key

Fingertips roam slowly over silken skin
Tingles ignite the want of heavenly sin
Bodies entwine in a moonlit dance
Eye to eye, this is a game of chance

Oneness, love and sin in your gaze
Lost in the deepness of your love for days
Emerging whole as never before
All because you passed through my door

I am standing on the inside, steady looking out
My heart belongs to you, of this I have no doubt.
Right now you are on the outside, even though part of
you is in.
Together we are waiting for the rest of our life to begin

Tears of Fate

Tears from heaven flow at times
When man needs the gift of hope
The water crystallizes in formations of joy
And falls to uncertain places

One pure thought he has for her
To hold her for time to come
Spend his moments in her thoughts
Emanations of two becoming one

Above the Earth collecting in a pattern of innocence
Blanketing in the purest form
In this sense she was his all along
Only to be claimed when he saw her face

The pace of life places Fate in our hand
Alighting to the gentle touch of a Lover who knows
Admiring her openly and following the quest
To win her heart as his own

She is like the snow that falls in April
The last of a kind and special to behold
Yours and at the same time- other's
Beautiful, she draws the wind to her side

Sunshine cannot force her form to melt- for she is mine
I hold her gaze from the Sun's rays
And have loved her for all time
As she has loved me all the days

The Sun drives a shift but not a rift
We are together and above it all
Before time began
Tears from heaven placed her in my hand

So she is mine and I am hers
And if rain melt the snow away
I'll find the uncertain place
And wait for that same day

Jenna Don't You Go

Love overcomes adversity and sorrow
With God's blessing there will be tomorrow
Hold onto your life with both your hands
Spend more time loving all your friends
Heal from all and awake refreshed
Count each day as being wonderfully blessed

Our thoughts and prayers
Come to you and cover softly like dew
On the petals of a lilly in the morning
Comforting and saving grace
Star gazing for all your days
Not cut short by mortality
But long in life as love
From Family and Friends

Jenna Don't You Go
Stay with us always
Be well and at peace
For what love is there
If the lilly closes?

Seeking Sibyl

Sibyl sees all as she peers stooped over supplicant and dreams
Black marble yields strength for her cause
And pleading eyes demand a future bright
She sees what she sees and it drains her color
The Center of the Universe takes its toll on her
Collapsing hope around her causes her to faint and tremble
Gaia's womb comforts but Apollo beats the war drum
As others seek to come to her eternal flame
That removes shadow and mist from the unknown
And days from her own life
Mount Parnassus in the Valley of Phocis tells a tale
Shrouded in stone and sternness
Phaedriades watches over the sorceress as she dooms and blesses
Those seeking tomorrow's secrets
Peril awaits many who seek while good fortune favors others
Does your fortitude allow for either as you ponder your fate?

While she peers into your heart to find what is unknown
to you
Clear to her with the insight of Apollo
Fear and reason are not oft married
Nor does hope follow the whim of those that ignore
The gift of not knowing
Seek Sibyl if you must
But rather seek the next step on the path of
righteousness?

Unless Hope Escape

Femme follows fire in deceit and dismay
Prometheus warned but unheeded that day
Unleashed torment from dire mistake
The seal of pithos loosed by Pandora and fate
Hesiod's tale was weaved with gifts from goddesses
Arced to earth from the heavens- like bolides aflame
Unleashed worship of Mammon from the misdeed of a
girl
Life and death interlace in a reflection of vane
incantations
Claiming happiness though sad when surrounded by
sorrow
Seeming gladness mists the eyes
Holding back the truth as Aphrodite and Hermes did from
her on that day of gifting
Works and Days- Ages of Man free from sin and strife
Filled now with doom and decay by actions that day
Wanting something else when you don't know what you
have
Zeus tampered with the flesh of man and lay Pandora in
his hand

Yearning deeply for knowledge she peered

All the world was turned for fear- demons poured from fountain frenzy

Filled our hearts with deadly deeds

And passed judgment on the free

Creating the need for hope

Blinding rain for all to see

Begging sunshine bliss to settle soundly

Perseverance conquers suffering profoundly

Epimetheus was sore pleased and from this hope was released

And unless hope escape its earthen vessel

How can man love woman?

I Will Survive (or 600 Steps)

Long ago I had a dream
Of wishes come true for you and me
It amazed me how so much could be right
In the day and in the night
I counted the steps to your house and was pleased it was
600
It was a perfect number
599 would get me to your door out of breath wanting to
see you
601 would get me to your door past patience and out of
control
600 made me want you just enough to hold you tight and
make you feel like the most important in the world
So 600 is just the right distance between us
So keep it so- don't move too far or too close

Other tracks marked the way
When I counted the 600 steps the other day
They were not my steps
Some were too light- they were made by someone who
did not take the journey to your door serious
Some were too heavy- they were more interested in their

own desire than yours

Some were an uneven pace- they wanted what they could get before you noticed their greed and selfishness

Others stopped to pause along the way- they were not sure of your love and charms

I ignored them- for my steps were just deep enough- I took my love for you serious

My pace was even- I was dedicated to your happiness and knew my mission and my heart's desire

There are no pauses in my gait- I am certain of my love for you

But the steps went to the same door as mine

Had they been let in?

I'll never look at the 600 steps the same again...

Maybe 800 is a better number?

Redheads Not Warheads

Whenever you need to move your heart to another
plateau
To graze on grass greener than any other
Or fill your lungs with laughter and charm
From another dream you might have had
It is best to find what you need under the Moon
The Sun burns too bright for open eyes
And the skin freckles in response
Pale is like a dream you could share with another

Anger washes over you like the water from the fall
Pouring through your hair
As you prepare for war and harm and cruelty
Anguish and sorrow come for you tomorrow
Take your lovers to your beds
Just for one night
Redheads Not Warheads

Awake prepared by love anon
To find an enemy and drive them from
What makes them happy and free
To captivity they flee

Take your lovers back to your beds
Redheads Not Warheads

Freedom comes at a price too high to pay
So close your eyes during the day
And pray that night will come soon
And claim what you have of worth
Blood on your hands looks like wine in the moonbeam
drama
Redwine and Redheads holding hands when dawn breaks
Complacent dreams make you miss the most

Awake prepared by love anon
Take from them what they cherish most
Drive them from their land
Wield a heavy hand, weighted with the languid prose of
destruction
Burn them where they sleep
Redwine washes the pain away
And Redheads cleanse your soul of turmoil and temerity
Redheads Not Warheads for another night

She moves like a flower in a breeze
Her face a backdrop for a dream
That plays for you in the gleam of her eyes

And it makes you cry
There is no war there for you to see
No pain or suffering
She holds your hand and draws you in
To a world of love and common friends
Redheads Not Warheads, every night

Despite

Even when you focus on perfection
And can describe it with abandon
Word for word descriptions of how things should be
Visions of what it looks like when it is built
These things are never enough
You underestimate the will of people to be unhappy
Despite what you'd do for them

Even when you care about every detail
And can focus on what needs to be done
You can feel the emotions wash over you
Communicate the desire for success
These things are never enough
You underestimate the will of people to fail
Despite handing them success

Even when you color the world in a rainbow of options
And write about the dream in prose and rhyme
And make it vivid with Technicolor vision
Share your passion for others
These things are never enough
You underestimate the people to be selfish
Despite being selfless

Even when you dedicate your time for the creations of something wonderful
Mix it with practicality and patience
Temper it with intelligence and ethical contribution
Educate others at their behest
These things are never enough
You underestimate the trend of a people to take you for granted
Despite being their friend

Even when you dedicate your work for their benefit
And provide excellence in every choice
Accompanied with loving care and kindness
Expand the vision to include their wants and concerns
These things are never enough
You underestimate their ability to be complacent in mediocrity
Despite bathing them in professionalism

Even when you try to learn from them
And never give up despite the desire to be like them
And quit when you don't get what you want
Or complain when it isn't right the first time
These things don't become you

You underestimate your ability to comprehend the weakness and frailty of people
Despite all your efforts

All the intentions in the world are not enough
Children cannot become great unless they will walk on their own
Take a step, fall, get up, and do it again
My children cry when they stumble
And I can't hear them cry
I underestimated my ability to hear the frequency of their failure
I have moved on and I won't look back to Sodom or Gomorrah

I know how to hold a path, even if I'm on it alone

She Wrote for Me

Many words have passed my pen
For those who draw the breath of men
And sharp these words that sting the skin
So much so, I'll not write again

Pain from more it cannot be
The words and thoughts have fled from me
I'll not write or think again
For those that take the breath of men

Drama drapes over my shoulder
And looks of contempt hurt and smolder
Igniting fire kindled by ire
Surrounded by lies and the mother liar

Exhausting thoughts pour from my mind
All the tempest I hold the line
I ink my blood in poetic praise
And it costs me life in weeks and days

When I gave my words to no one else
And practiced silence and earnest stealth
A braided woman I did not see
Took some time and wrote for me

The words were soft and warm to feel
Made me hope again and reel
The words can pour out from my pen
For those who take the breath of men, again

Heliopolis

Apexing the delta and the Nile, the City sits empty
Nestled in Augustamnica province holding Cleopatra's
Needle
The Pillars stand alone now- waiting for companionship
Actis, Son of Helios and Rhode built well but cannot
sustain the life
Necessary to fill the streets with laughter and mirth
Ptolemy's reign occupied the walls and halls for a time
And even now some approach- walking through lotus
fields
Nymphaea lotus, Nymphaea cerulean, and Nelumbo
nucifera
Closed at night and underwater- exposed by day to
Amun-Ra
Obelisks in patches of overgrown grass surrounded by
sand
Lead the way to Heliopolis Reborne
Entering the City transforms and resurrects you
Horus fed the masses with bread before and will soon
again
Mouths of gods and goddesses approach nearer still

Amun-Ra notes their approach with waves of sunlit empathy
Alexander stopped on his way from Pelusium to Memphis
Drawn by the warmth of the people and magic in the air
Their tracks in the sand will pause at the gates before they enter
To bring life and love to the City of Pillars once again
Heliopolis will never be the same- and it doesn't want to be

Above It All

Overhead and holding steady, Amun-Ra purveys
Rays of sunlight wash the city in a newness not seen for
days
Heliopolis called forth to awakened gods of yesterday
And they heed its' beckoning call
Once more relevant and powerful
It is the City of the Sun once again
Son of Earth and Sky appears below
Calling out in song to Sister Isis
Waking her from soulful slumber and her simplicity
Queen of Heaven – Mother of the Gods
Nepthys, Completer of her Sister, follows quietly
Disturbing not the dead nor the lotus flowers under foot
Her entrance to the city as the Lady of the Temple
creates hope
And as the priests return they can worship and adore
Once more under the watchful gaze of Ra
The Citie's Breath returns anew, Serket is a windy
presence
Protecting Love and City with Aset and Nebet Het
Her Sisters in the City wake and sing in harmony

The Lioness Protector makes her way to Heliopolis
As if called by the song of the ages
Ancient rites and rituals called forth as flames peak and peer
Shadows roam the homes of many who return
Senwosret is made whole at the obilisk where they meet
Holding hands, eyes focused on the heat above
Re-Hekarte appeased as the city lives and hope returns
Ra peers from above and his lingering rays may burn
Indifference yields a passive care as his attention shifts

Pain and a (Ship Wreck)

The tale of a man and his folly lost at sea in a tempest of imperfection, lost confidence, and enough remorse for a lifetime

Crashing down all around me
My feelings are like rubble in the city center
Tragic fortune has fallen fast
And my resolve's not built to last

(The ship is pushed off course by the wind and waves
The crew is lost and they don't know it
Land is near but not to be found
The ship will sink or run aground)

Speeding by when I'm not watching
Pain is my companion on this journey
Even though I travel alone and quiet
It wasn't always quite this way

(The white caps tell of danger hidden
The sailors doom by maidens bidden
The rutter hard astern to pass
The crash like shattered bone and dermaplast)

There were better times and happier days
Long ago and maybe not really mine at all
Might have seen them flash in a nighttime sky
And hoped what I saw was meant for me

(Swimming for shore that's not in sight
Fighting for life with all his might
Viscious death makes him wet
It's not the water- but regret)

Anguish – Solitude – Remorse
All the waters have dried and the lake is barren
No more to give and no one to take
A heart of hope and stone about to break

(Water soaked and heavy laden
Siren call from fairest maiden
He follows her voice to deeper water
Face-to-face with Poseidon's daughter)

No tears are shed the angel has fallen
No eyes to watch the dream is over
No words to say his hope is broken
His attention's fake and patience token

(He no longer swims but is afloat bundled with his sins
Pushed by wave and wind
He hears a faint voice on the distance
But remembers he has no friends)

Moving on and moving faster
His dream has become a sad disaster
No longer servant or even master
Can't you feel his peace destroyed?

(Take me, watery grave you are my friend
Drown me fast and make it end
Put me down were I belong
Fill my lungs with liquid punishment- end my song)

He won't give- so take
Not one piece- so break
And get away from the whole in my heart
Your fingers tear it wide apart

(Memories pass before the flicker leaves his mind
Some are harsh and others kind
One stands out above the others
He has no sisters and no brothers)

Alone at last- he started like that anyway
By himself- another day
Built to last? Not today
Maybe tomorrow- filled with sorrow

(Dead at last, alone again
River crossed with one new friend
Coins in his hand to pay his toll
Will darkness even take his soul?)

Let me be alone with my mistakes
We keep each other fast and warm
Call each other familiar names
And embrace softly in our doom

(Rejected even after death
A common tale so we know the rest
Pity fallen on an empty field
A man without his sword or shield)

Mistake, my mistress and my friend
The only one I comprehend
She keeps the knife against my throat
The blood drops stain all my purest hopes

(Naked and alone
Words hold him in place
His own words he reads for
No one writes for him)

Dramatic words or heartfelt woes?
Passing memories or lifetime throes?
If he finds he knows she goes
Inside his heart where no one knows

(The bitter end starring hard
Like work when you are tired
His talent caught and mired
In human frailty and missed marks)

He won't go and he won't stay
He'll just be something like a shadow
Of what he used to be
And it will be enough- he doesn't want anything anyway

(In time he will be good once more
And in that moment he will realize
What he had lost
And weep all over again)

He will close his eyes to hide his tears
And forget the time to hide the years
And fake a smile to hold the fears
He won't sound like himself- so get used to it

(Let me have a private shame
Read this poem- forget my name
Don't offer kindness or ask for blame
From king to pawn in someone's game
Don't look at me- I'm not the same)

The sun was too bright anyway
So I'll just stand in the shade

Past Pandemonium

It's been too long since the fire started to burn
It's been so long I don't know where to turn
Will you be there when the night starts to fall?
Will you be there when I need you most of all?

It's past pandemonium when you call my name
Without your words on my ear life isn't the same
Don't stop looking for me to come
Don't stop in case I am the one

There are rules that are given in life
Some you can and others you can't ignore
Have we been down this road before?
And if we have, is this a different door?

Sleep...Baby...Sleep
Dream of how we used to be together
Before the rain started falling and life was just
Another front and Stormy Weather

I'll braid your hair and try to make fourteen minutes work
I'll hold you hand and carry your books

I'll watch your eyes and hope to catch
A lover's look and smile and the hope of love requited

I'll hide my love behind Greek tragedy
And promise eternity in hopes you'll come to me
I'll launch poetic wonderment and call you Venus
I'll use quantum theory to shrink the space between us

I'll feel your loss when you've lost something
And I'll cry when you lay awake at night
I'll hope you love me and dream that we
Hold each other tight at night and in the light

I'll write of one thousand ships
And beauty beyond compare
I'll weave ringlets in your hair
With the purest lover's care

I'll follow and dance and sing to you
Watch you walk and sit under the moon
I'll talk all night and swing next to you
There is nothing by your side that I won't do

We are past pandemonium
And approaching sanctity with the stars

At light speed and holding hands
In a blur of gravity we become one

Mixed in myth and legend and lore
Composite love and hardened core
Divine intervention and collateral damage
With our love we break barriers and silences and awaken
hopes

I've felt your touch when others couldn't
And seen your face when others hadn't
I've known your love when I probably shouldn't
And I give my self when I said I wouldn't

Turning left at uncertainty and pausing for life's cross
traffic
Looking at the scenery for landmarks familiar
Finding none and lost again
We'll make it home but we don't know when

Aphrodite would cease to be Aphrodite
And Paris would set Helen free
If that is what it takes alas
To keep you here with me
For we are past pandemonium

Her

Before he met Her…

Azure memories in a cloudy sky
Saturated falling down and sadly
Dawn breaks over a lake of frigid tears
Glistening over all those lost years

Dusty dreams on parched lips
Aims for lust but mostly missed
Seeing darkness all around
Lost hope paves the ground

Sullen and melancholy laughter
Echoes through a forest of grand trees
Thoughts of charismatic wonder
Fall slowly like feathers in a breeze

Then he met Her…

Colliding like two storms in a lake
Waves crash together making Stormy weather
Oscillations and ominous ramifications
They mix their essence becoming one
The perfect storm

Amethyst dreams in a Sunshine sky
Lofty praise floats dreamily by
Moonshine on a calm lake
Highlighting promise and eternity

Hopes quench a thirst
Love and Lust accompany falling stars
Expanse of light softly covers
The way ahead is clear and sure

Joy ripples the water's surface
Playing symphonies of wonder
Jubilation and excitation hold hands
And fly away free

Because he met Her...

The Way It Could Have Been

If I was a boy in your school…

Unencumbered I can wonder
If the present were torn sunder
What would change about the past
If only I had you to ask
"May I carry your books, Dear?"

To travel back to times ago
And find a present undiscovered
Seeing you in brightest bloom
Right next to your beauty I hovered
"May I sit by you, Dear?"

Many thoughts one can possess
About even the morrow
But yesterday is on my mind
More so than tomorrow
"May I hold your hand, Dear?"

Beyond the veil and mist of sorrow
I have a dream of another morrow
Different than the one today

We meet in a nearby park to play
"May I swing with you, Dear?"

Looking through a different window
Than the one right by my chair
I see you standing in my driveway
Pretty ribbon in your hair
"Come and talk with me, Dear?"

Seeing clearly what was shadowed
Tasting love that's now forbidden
My feelings are no longer hidden
Thoughts of you my mind is ridden
"Come and kiss my lips, Dear?"

Taking what is offered, gladly
Loving you so very, madly
Not seeing you strikes me, sadly
Be with you I must, and badly
"Hold onto me forever, Dear?"

Today is here just like before
But I have you now and so much more
I have your books and hand in mine

We brought with us a perfect time

"See you on the morrow, Dear."

The Quark and the Girl

A quark is a generic type of physical particle that forms one of the two basic constituents of matter, the other being the lepton. Various species of quarks combine in specific ways to form protons and neutrons, in each case taking exactly three quarks to make the particle in question.

There are six different types of quark, usually known as flavors: up, down, charm, strange, top, and bottom.

Strange
A world devoid of a girl like her
Would be Strange indeed
For when we have a girl like her
She's all a boy would need

Charm
The world will reel and wobble
From my lover's Charm
And when you see her beauty
You'd have her on your arm

Top
When it comes to class and alacrity

She is at the Top
Her meteor is quickly rising
And I don't think that it'll stop

Bottom
When it comes to selfish pride and haste
You know she hasn't got them
For when you look upon that list
She's always at the Bottom

Up
Life has its Ups and downs
There is no life without them
But with a girl like her around
Only ups you'll find then

Down
She is joy unconstrained
Floating on a cloud of mirth
But when she sees me coming
She settles Down to earth

Your Impact is Infinite

Wisdom measured in words
Love in purest action
Oneness in time together
And raw satisfaction

If the wind blew through your hair
It would stop and caress each strand
As if it found an enchanting home
In some wondrous and magical land

If the sun kissed your lips
It would pause its heavenly travel
Lingering at that sweet contact
Its ball would soon unravel

If the moon met your gaze
It would soon melt away
There'd be nothing left of it
To hold the waters in their sway

If the stars could sense your touch
They'd twinkle just for you
And follow you in your walks
Like one in love would do

If the universe could somehow know your love
The simple would become intricate
For when in the focus of your love
Your impact is impossibly infinite

When You Lose Something You Shouldn't

There is no blame when you've done nothing wrong
Like pick the wrong words when writing a song
Or when something goes that should have stayed
Nothing to do when things go this way

Pain and regret wash over your soul
Makes you feel broken and far less than whole
Comfort will come as soon as it can
For all things that happen follow a plan

Those who love you share in your pain
And wish that this sorrow never visits again
Desire to take your hurt but we couldn't
When my dear you've lost something you shouldn't

Be at peace knowing that right
Will be by your side through the days and the nights
And as you stop looking for that which was lost
It will be found again no matter the cost

Those who think about you day and night
Want to make this tale turn out right
Desiring to take your hurt but we couldn't
When my dear you've lost something you shouldn't

Sky at Night

In the sky tonight
We see swirling sheaths of light
Dancing to a heavenly harmonic
Christening the dark blue sky
With swirls of incandescent purples and pinks
An aerial trapeze between stars of wonder
While we watch the moon loom over our embrace

Darkness paints a backdrop for the show
Stars scattered across the sky- to and fro
The moon comes to us and dances in our laps
Keeping us company while we talk
Starlight reflecting off evening dew
Keeping your face from shadow
Painting your beauty for the heavens

Nebulous whispers in your ear from me and the night sky
Words of affection transferred between you and I
Under the glow of mighty grandeur
A comet crosses between constellations and
consternations
The heavens reel from the mighty discharge
Lightning jumps from cloud to cloud

Collapsing vacuums crashing loud
The vision is euphoric as it plays out overhead
Unfolding drama for our pleasure
As we sit and talk together

In the sky tonight and in your eyes
I see the purples and pinks with your own greens
Translated cosmic energy and I know what it means
You are mine while the heavens fight their fall
You are mine but that's not all
The sky is ours and dances to please
And weaves a poem with its breeze
And finishes with your smile

The Hand That Rocks the Cradle Rules the World

Their love for us makes the world go 'round
They pick us up and set us down
They hold our hand and protect our steps
Their strength in us one day begets
A strength and power of our own
As we leave our mother's home

For from the time you come till the time you leave
She prays for you down on her knees
You come before any desire she possesses
She wears her love for you like long tresses
She will fight for you as need be
She will see for you when you can't see
She will speak for you when you know not what to say
And her wisdom will often guide your way (at least it
should)
Stand by your side when others might not
When you have nothing—she's all you've got
She directs your steps to success
And prays your days be many and blessed

She seconds herself for you
In a world where selfishness rules

She gives up her life as no other would

So your life will be as it should (as she intended it)

She is your Mother

The Hand That Rocks the Cradle

The Hand That Rules the World

She is your Mother

And with her—you need no other

Red Flowers

You deserve something of beauty
To compliment your own
Although it doesn't exactly match
The idea is not alone

Wild like the love we share
Red as the passion of heated skin
Hold these in remembrance of me
Until we are one again

A Day Above All Others

Some days come and go without much to remember
Everything just seems a blur
Like most of the month of December

Some days feel like all the rest
There isn't any differentiation
All you do is tread and tread
And try to keep your station

Some days are way too long
They just never seem to end
And when you thought it over
You wake to do it all again

Sometimes there is a chance
For a special day to come
Even in a life time
There will only be the one

I have one of those to tell you about:

She is beauty beyond compare
And so lovely to behold
And with word and ceremony
She is forever mine to love and hold

She is stormy perfection
A symphony to ponder
Like a honey laced confection
With a tidal wave of wonder

She stood with me and made a vow
To be with me forever
So now I know no matter what
We will always be together

I love her with all my being
And she is in love with me
As the days pass slowly by
Our love is bound in certainty

A Day Above All Others
When she gave herself to me
Solidified our eternal love
"I was made to be with thee"

We were together
As One – A Miracle
Woven in a single tapestry
And then we watched the water...

That's My Day Above All Others

Bound Together

We are bound together
Like stars in a constellation
Marked upon the heavens
By this earthly celebration

We are bound together
In life, love, and deed
I will provide for you
Every want and need

We are bound together
By a thread between our souls
And as we commit our love
The thread will surely grow

We are bound together
That truth rings so clear
My eternal hope and desire
Is to always have you near

An Angel with Silver Wings

She masters many things
Beauty not least of all
And she carries hope and love
Enough to head the call
Of love between them both

She gives more than takes
Bends before breaks
Smiles over frowns
More ups and less downs
And she has silver wings

She puts him first
To love and to cherish
Sacrifices herself– so he won't perish
Willing to give
So that he might live
And she has silver wings

She holds him up
When he might fall
She answers sweetly

When she hears his call
She holds him tight
When he's wrong or he's right
And she has silver wings

She warms his heart
When he is cold
She doesn't fret or let it get old
She kisses softly
When he needs affection
She keeps her eyes
Always in his direction
And she has silver wings

She masters many things
His heart not least of all
And he answers sweetly
When he hears her gently call
His angel appears to him
When he needs her close
From nearby– so fast appearing
His pulse quickens
She is nearing

To be with him now and forever
They will always be together

And She Has Silver Wings

Morning Glory

Love is invisible to most
But not to all
Some can see the telling whisper of kindness
Or the ghost of a loving glance
Or sense the remembrance of a touch shared
Possibly see the trail of pollen on the table
From the flowers he gave her yesterday
Even see colored paper—torn and broken
From a gift given in love
See the flicker in someone's eyes when they meet those
of their lover
Love isn't invisible to all
Just to most

Love is silent to most
But not to all
Some hear the whisper of a lover
Maybe see the trail of a loving phrase
Or sense the tone he uses with his Love
Perceive the faint echoes of "I love you" and "I love you
too"
Feel the reverberation of a kiss that was just right

Embracing tight causes shivers a butterfly can sense
Listen to a message left wishing her a great day
When his was bad and getting worse
Love isn't silent to all
Just to most

Love is cold to most
But not to all
Maybe feel the heat of a long touch
Or the fire passion kindles
Radiation that desire puts in the air
And the warmth from a loving look
The heat when two bodies touch
Long enough but not—at the same time
The heat between me and you
The fire started by windswept walks on a beach
Love isn't cold to all
Just to most

So you can see love if you look
You can hear love if you listen
In the morning love is like Sunshine on a cold field
It warms and brings to life
Those in the glow

Morning Glory
That's Love's Story

Majestic Trees

Slowly reaching towards the heavens
Like so many of us with our lofty thoughts
As they reach up they provide shade and comfort
To those below
While we drag others along as if we must
They spread wide their arms and embrace all
While we cling to what belongs to us
They allow rest for the weary
We drive to the brink of exhaustion
And then continue on
They fill the sky with life and movement
We take and use and consume and destroy
They root to the earth in collaboration
While we command and conquer
We have so much to learn from them
It is a shame we burn them to be
A shame we consume them to prosper
While they give to us from what they have to give
And have enough to last with dignity
Until life collapses under the burden of taxation
Caused by corruption and condemnation

We are majesty

And They are Majestic All the While

Happy Clouds

Watery wisps dance a waltz
Of wonderful remembrance and playful exuberance
As they paint for joy and those who know to look
At the drama of creativity unfolding overhead
Do they smile at me when I look?
Do they dance for me?
The patterns they make tell stories from long ago
And tomorrow
Of love and hope and sometimes sorrow
These clouds are different- they tell a new tale
They form shapes of mirth and music
And cause the eyes to dance to their tune
Drifting from form to form
Shaped by unseen forces
Drawn to them by the beauty of it all
Darting from east to west and touching birds and blue
sky
As they pass by
These clouds are content in their imaginary realm
Tracing life as we see it and telling us they see it too
Sharing our time by offering humor

For me to laugh at
And if you are quiet
You can hear then laugh with you as well
For they are Happy Clouds

Sunshine at Sunset

Your whispers make the waters still
A liquid canvas to reflect the sun's warmth towards heaven
I am bathed by that warming reflection when I am with you
Your gentle breath parts the vapors coalesced
And moves them to and fro
Detailing the sky with patterns of hope and serenity
Providing a comfort akin to the peace you share with me when I am by your side
Resting on the ocean still, an island, the foundation for the love I have for you—and you for me
The rays of sunlight scattered through the clouds are the joy and mirth you bring to me when I see your face and hear your voice
The blue sky is the backdrop for your beauty- pure and unblemished
You are the sun as it shines down on me
Through the cloudy skies
You warm my soul and set my path
You are Magnificence set in Beauty

Found at the Longitude of Perfection
And the Latitude of Bliss
A perfect wonder for the world and my imagination
A Girl for My Time and Contemplations
A Girl for Me
You are Sunshine at Dusk
You are Sunshine at Dawn
You are Sunshine at Sunset

Her Lips Require Special Care

He knelt beside his lover
And watched her quietly
With the softest of touches he brought finger tip to skin
Gently above the surface but close enough to feel her
beauty
Slowly etching each contour and feature of her face
Her lips require special care
For sometimes his own lips are there
Her neck is slightly cool
Near her heart but far enough
To fill the chill of the nighttime air
He traces her shoulder and his breath disturbs her hair
With the faintest of hesitations he moves in and down
Caressing her breast without making a sound
He slowly smiles and deeply breathes in
And he found what he anticipated
The wound he left is cold and coagulated
In the moonlight his face betrays emaciation
His hunger ate the love
And in that single fit of rage he pierced his purest dove

O to be a Dream

O to be a dream
Never disappointing
Because you are never what you seem
Imagined as the most wondrous
A tempest of delight
To spin and twirl
In your lover's mind
Each and every night

A knight if she supposes
Polite in all the docile poses
Ever equipped with roses
Protecting her maidenhood anew
All these things and more
Each night as she dreams of you
As the plot continues- the night wanes to dawn

She moves to kiss nocturnal wish
And the clamor rages on
It's 6 o'clock
The sun is up
And the man of her dreams is gone
Not far it seems- but down the hall
To let the dogs out on the lawn

Remarkably Commonplace

I suppose that in deep repose
Once could possibly cogitate
And I'd decry as soon as defy
The inescapable pull of gravity

One day perchance
In a fit of happenstance
O to see honest depravity
Bite down if you wish
Crush your teeth on a dish
And expose the blight and the cavity

If you persist
You might get what you wished
If only you knew with certainty
What it was that you needed
Before need receded
And left you alone with absurdity

I suppose that in deep repose
Once could possibly contemplate
And I'd decry as soon as defy
That alone is remarkably commonplace

And the Thrill is Gone

Sing song wailing and the thrill is gone
He wanted revenge but he knew it was wrong
Temptation screaming his name in rhythm
All alone on his death bed and prison
Raven eyes pierce the night
Black on black and cold as ice
Trembling in anticipation
Mumbling the curse of desecration
Clutching hope in desperation
Tasting blood he swallows his tongue
Right is right and wrong is wrong
Sing song wailing and the thrill is gone

Once in past not long ago
A battle was lost against that aged foe
Tossed and torn to and fro
He cried for peace and was told "No"

Sing song wailing and the thrill is gone
She stabbed her dad and burned her mom
She knew it was wrong but didn't care
Clutching at her mother's hair
Sorrow won't come near this child
Her fear is old and living wild

Temptation screams her name in rhythm
All alone on her death bed and prison
The raven quiets its neck is wrung
Tasting blood she swallows her tongue
Right is right and wrong is wrong
Sing song wailing and the thrill is gone

Once in past not long ago
A battle was lost against that aged foe
Tossed and torn to and fro
She cried for peace and was told "No"

Courage

It comes without warning

As the sun rises in the morning

And as the sun heats the surface of the glass

Do it now or it will pass

The cracks shape your future

The picture is no longer clear

The jagged edge of latent fear

Changes hope to regret each year

While the glass is warm it's clear

Do it now and flee your fear

Turn discourage into a voyage

Across time and space

Venture into the netherworld where

Hope is much more commonplace

If it passes you'll wish you held onto the wake

And in the noonday sun the glass will break

The pieces cannot be forged again

Assume the courage and help your friend

Anymore

Take me places where the waters kiss the sand

Holding my love in the palm of your hand

There are no bitter tears

In this forlorn and forsaken land

But we haven't got one anymore

The water carried it from the shore

Deep water and despair

I see it sinking over there

The sea salt dissolves the text

I fear it comes for my soul next

Salvations not hear anymore

The water carried it from the shore

Take me places where the waters kiss the sand

Holding on hand-to-hand

There are frozen years

Coldest heart and solid tears

The sun will thaw it all one day

But not before we're carried away

A Spiral Galaxy and Depravity

Waves of light washing over me

Andromeda strain and depravity

Pulled to you by fate and rapidly

The only girl in my galaxy

Pulse and plenum

Gravitational duodenum

Pulled to you by fate and vapidly

The only girl in my galaxy

Shifting closer

Spinning continuity

Repelled and dense

A common calamity

Refuge from a tempestuous sea

Drowning in blue rhapsody

It's mostly just you and me

Handstanding into eternity

Starry Night

Calling in the void transparently

Where she lands and sleeps tonight

Ends every time catastrophically

But it's late and she dries

The spiral tears in his eyes

Staining the conceit of man

And she holds the world in her hand

Petals in the Breeze

Every day the world revolves

And carries you in its grasp

Leaving another multiverse

Alone, white and aghast

Brightest embers burn

Effervescent just the same

The wind calling in rhyme-

Each letter of your name

Petals in the breeze

Fragrant in the rain

Ever calling in close whisper

Never placing blackest blame

Circles and chords of hope

Abandon nearest splendor

Ringlets of fiery abandon

Laughter sings a tune and lingers

Another set of days go by

And a ring upon your finger

(the color of the blood)

It might be over when the clouds catch fire
It might be colder when you climb higher
It might be
(depends on the color of the blood)

You could talk to me and I would hear
You could cry with me and share your tears
You could
(depends on the color of the blood)

Tantalizing scream and scintillating dream
Sudden silence as you enter the scene
You slip and fall and crack your skull
The brilliant blaze of infinity

It will feel hollow when the ache is on
It will be painful when the love is gone
It will
(depends on the color of the blood)

It should last all the years
It should scatter all the fears
It should
(depends on the color of the blood)

Enthralling shine wishing you were mine
Vacuum and boom right before the crime
You slip and impale your heart
In the crown of light just before the dark

(depends on the color of the blood)

YOU NEVER KNOW

www.ingramcontent.com/pod-product-compliance
Lightning Source LLC
Chambersburg PA
CBHW060329100426
42812CB00003B/928